HIS HEALING HANDS

Finding God in Broken Places

MARGARET FEINBERG

FOREWORD BY SHEILA WALSH

THOMAS NELSON
Since 1798

NASHVILLE   DALLAS   MEXICO CITY   RIO DE JANEIRO

Published in Nashville, Tennessee, by Thomas Nelson. Thomas Nelson is a trademark of Thomas Nelson, Inc.

Thomas Nelson, Inc., titles may be purchased in bulk for educational, business, fund-raising, or sales promotional use. For information, please e-mail SpecialMarkets@ ThomasNelson.com.

All Scripture quotations are taken from THE NEW KING JAMES VERSION. © 1982 by Thomas Nelson, Inc. Used by permission. All rights reserved.

Page design: Crosslin Creative

978-1-4016-7625-4

Printed in the United States of America

13 14 15 16 17 RRD 5 4 3 2 1

Contents

Foreword

I remember the sinking feeling that I had in the pit of my stomach as waves of disbelief assaulted me. My mom loved this vase. She loved it for many reasons. She loved the delicate porcelain, so fine it was almost translucent in the sunlight. She loved the tiny bluebells that had been hand-painted by a careful and gifted artist. But most of all, she loved the fact that it had been handed down to her from her mother who had in turn received it from her mother. Now it lay in what seemed like a million pieces on the unforgiving linoleum that covered the kitchen floor. There was nothing I could do. It was clear that the vase could not be glued back together as the devastation was too complete. I considered my options.

1. Run away from home

2. Await the return of Christ and pray that it was imminent

3. Tell my mom what I had done

Option one was tempting but as I was only ten years old it seemed a bit out of my league. Option two was extraordinarily appealing but as far as I could tell, God was not on board with this option. There was only one option left. I told my cat, Tiger, that I loved her and prepared for option three. I found my mother in the garden pruning roses and almost turned around as she was wielding what seemed to be a lethal weapon, but it was now or never.

"Mom, you know the vase that has been passed from generation to generation," I began. "Well, this generation just dropped it!"

I don't honestly remember now what my mom said or did, but what I do remember is the feeling of hopelessness as I saw the extent of the brokenness. Little did I understand as a child that that physical reality would be played out in my life in years to come, not with a porcelain vase, but with my fragile heart.

I wonder if you have been there too?

This study is on brokenness and what God alone can do with broken hearts and broken lives. As a ten-year-old girl I longed to be able to hide the pieces of my mom's treasured vase but in time they would have been found. So too as an adult, I longed to hide my brokenness from others and from God Himself but time revealed the cracks. I know now that brokenness is a gift, for as Samuel Chadwick once wrote, "It's amazing what God can do with a broken heart if you bring Him all the pieces."

That is my prayer for you, dear sister, as you begin the study. I pray you will be amazed by the love of God and by His healing hands.

> But we have this treasure in earthen vessels, that the excellence of the power may be of God and not of us. We are hard-pressed on every side, yet not crushed; we are perplexed, but not in despair; persecuted, but not forsaken; struck down, but not destroyed—always carrying about in the body the dying of the Lord Jesus, that the life of Jesus also may be manifested in our body. . . . Therefore we do not lose heart. Even though our outward man is perishing, yet the inward man is being renewed day by day. For our light affliction, which is but for a moment, is working for us a far more exceeding and eternal weight of glory. (2 Corinthians 4:7–10, 16, 17)

—Sheila Walsh

Introduction

Leaving No Stone Unturned

The LORD is near to those who have a broken heart, and saves such as have a contrite spirit.

Psalm 34:18

God specializes in impossible situations. When we find ourselves struggling to hold on to hope, wondering where the much-needed provision will come from, or even doubting that real change is possible, God meets us there. Whatever challenges we're facing, God longs to wrap His arms of love around us and bring healing. Nothing is beyond His grip.

This is God's nature. When it comes to redemption, God leaves no stone unturned. No fragment of brokenness escapes His notice. God wants to bring wholeness to every area of our lives.

When did you last notice an area in your soul that didn't feel quite right? Maybe you thought an event from the past was history until a particular conversation reminded you that the pains from all those years ago still remain. Or maybe you're in a situation right now and you feel a dull ache or sharp twinge in the pit of your stomach every time you think about the details.

We all have areas in our lives where we're broken. These broken places may be fragments of events in the past or a result of circumstances in the present, and their presence reminds us of our need for healing and restoration. The incredible news of being a child of God is that everything we need to experience healing is available to us. God not only wants to meet us in the midst of our brokenness, God wants to extend His healing hands to us.

God's passionate desire for wholeness, restoration, and provision is demonstrated repeatedly throughout the life, death, and resurrection of Jesus Christ. Through His earthly ministry, Jesus met people who had let go of hope, faced impossible situations, and waited in desperate need of a Savior. Throughout the Gospels, we encounter stories of Jesus meeting people right where they are and performing mighty miracles in response to their needs. These stories of Jesus—whether calming the storm, feeding the crowds, paying a hefty tax bill, or reaching out to those on the margins—give us the hope and faith that, as Jesus met others in areas of deep needs, He will also meet us.

Throughout this study, we'll look at different stories from the Gospels of Matthew, Mark, Luke, and John—all of which describe tender moments of Jesus meeting people in their brokenness. My hope and prayer is that as you read and reflect on these stories you'll find yourself experiencing God right in the midst of your brokenness. And as you do, may you feel the embrace of God's healing hands in your life.

Blessings,
Margaret Feinberg

God Meets Us in the Broken Places

God meets us in
the broken places.
God finds us when
the storms of life roll
in, when we feel like
we're at the end of our rope,
and when we're between a
rock and a hard place. No
matter what situation you're in,
God wants to meet you there
and wrap His loving arms
around you.

People thrash about in seas of guilt, anger,
despair. Life isn't working. We are going
down fast. But God can rescue us. And only
one message matters. His! We need to see
God's glory.

Max Lucado,
Popular author and pastor

When the Storms of Life Roll In

Calming the Storm

One can only imagine the excitement and joy one of Jesus'
followers, Peter, feels when he learns that Jesus is coming to his
home to meet his family. The long awaited Messiah, the Promised
One of Israel, is about to enter his house.

Passing through the doorway, Jesus doesn't comment on the
décor, the size, or the layout of the living area. Instead, Jesus'
focus draws toward one woman: Peter's mother-in-law. Lying sick
in bed with a fever, she likely spends much of the day shivering
from the cold one moment and sweating from heat the next.
Though she feels bad, she probably looks worse.

At the sound of Peter's voice, she may crane her neck—even
call out to him. Scripture doesn't record such details. Instead,
the text zeroes in on Jesus' response to this sick woman. Jesus

doesn't say a word: He simply touches her hand and the fever is gone in an instant.

Everyone watches in awe of the miracle that's just taken place. Some likely smile; others laugh with joy.

How does the woman respond to the miracle?

Matthew 8:15 tells us, "She arose and served them."

This woman's response to the miraculous healing in her life is service toward Jesus. What an extraordinary act!

Later that evening as Peter's family and Jesus' followers gather around, those who are sick and possessed by evil spirits are brought to Jesus. He heals them one by one.

Shortly after, Jesus and His disciples leave by boat to cross to the other side of the Sea of Galilee, a giant lake in the northern region of Israel. Likely exhausted by the day's events, Jesus falls asleep. A great storm brews. The wind starts blowing. The gusts grow stronger. Whitecaps form. The next thing the disciples know, the waves crash over the bow of the small boat.

> "Why are you fearful, O you of little faith?"
> (Matthew 8:26)

Even the most seaworthy of Jesus' followers grow fearful for their lives. They wake Jesus and beg Him to save them—convinced they're going to die.

Jesus' response is startling: "Why are you fearful, O you of little faith?" (Matthew 8:26).

The disciples believe they're about to perish, and Jesus replies with a simple question. Then He stands up, instructs the winds and sea to be quiet, and in an instant everything calms. The wind dies, the sea becomes glassy, and the disciples are left to marvel at the wonder they've just witnessed.

These stories are found in Matthew 8:14–27, and they demonstrate Jesus' ability to calm multiple storms. For Peter's mother-in-law, the storm of sickness left her weak, ill, and most likely wondering if she'd get better. Those who were sick or possessed by evil spirits probably wondered along with their families whether the storms in their lives would ever end. And the disciples were convinced they were going to die because of the wind and storm clouds overhead. Yet in every situation, Jesus calmed the storm—bringing His healing touch and restoration and demonstrating His power as the Son of God. Indeed, God is bigger and more powerful than any storm we will ever face.

1. When the storms of life roll in, how do you tend to respond?

2. In one sentence or phrase, share one of the most difficult storms you've weathered. What role did Christ play in getting through that difficult time? In addition to Christ, what made the difference in getting through that storm of life?

While Peter's mother-in-law's fever may have easily been broken with the use of ibuprofen today, a fever in ancient times was far less predictable and usually indicated a much more severe illness, like malaria, which lacked any cure. Jesus performed a miracle by restoring the mother-in-law to full health instantaneously with a simple touch.

The profundity of the moment is not to be missed. In ancient times women were often marginalized. Yet Jesus crossed social boundaries to heal Peter's mother-in-law, extending His love well beyond cultural norms.

3. Read **Matthew 8:14, 15**. How did Peter's mother-in-law express her gratitude to Jesus for calming the storm of sickness in her life and bringing healing? How do you tend to show gratitude for the moments when the storms of your life are calmed?

The Greek word for "serve" in verse 15 is *diakoneo*. The word suggests that the response went beyond Peter's mother-in-law providing a meal and expressed gratitude toward Jesus.

✣ ✣ ✣

When people learned Jesus was in town, they began bringing to Him those who were possessed by evil spirits and those who were sick. With only words, Jesus began healing them.

4. Read **Matthew 8:16, 17**. What does this passage reveal about Jesus' power over evil?

Matthew quoted Isaiah 53:4 in verse 17. Isaiah 53 is known as a servant song, which alludes to the Messiah coming as a servant to take on our suffering as His own. In quoting this verse, Matthew was proclaiming Jesus as the Messiah or the Christ. "Messiah" is the Hebrew word for *anointed one*, whereas "Christ" means *anointed one* in Greek.

✣ ✣ ✣

After healing the sick and demon possessed, Jesus and His disciples climbed into a boat to head for the other side of the Sea of Galilee. Many of those who stepped in the boat were familiar with the waters—they'd grown up fishing on the Sea of Galilee and crossed this freshwater lake countless times over the years. The Sea of Galilee is renowned for its size, thirteen miles long and eight miles wide, as well as its elevation, seven hundred feet below sea level.

5. Read **Matthew 8:23–27**. How did Jesus' response to the storm compare and contrast to the disciples' response to the storm? List the differences in their respective circles and the similarity in the intersecting part of the circles. (Hint: To figure out the similarity, see Matthew 8:25. What did the disciples expect Jesus to do, and what did Jesus know all along He could do?)

Jesus' Response   **Disciples' Response**

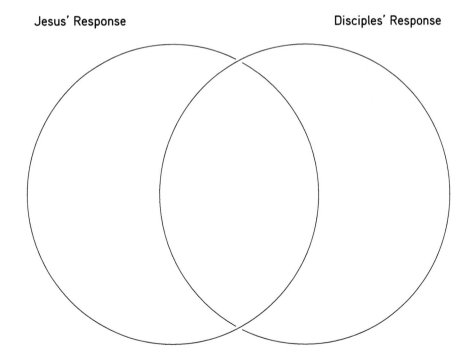

Jesus and His followers crammed into a boat to cross the sea. A boat during Jesus' time would have held as many as sixteen passengers—four rowers and one rudder man made up the crew.

6. Jesus revealed His power over disease (healing Peter's mother-in-law), power over the invisible world (casting out the evil spirits), and power over nature (calming the storm). Which of these areas is the most challenging for you to trust Jesus within your own life?

In the book of Jonah, God also demonstrated His power over the storm. Jonah was instructed by God to speak out against the bad behavior taking place in an infamous city called Nineveh. Rather than obey, Jonah ran the opposite direction. He found a ship heading to Tarshish and jumped on board. While out at sea, a great storm overwhelmed the ship, but Jonah didn't notice because he was sound asleep. When those aboard discovered Jonah caused the storm due to his disobedience, they were understandably upset. Jonah suggested they toss him overboard. Though the plan sounded cockamamie, they finally agreed.

7. Read **Jonah 1:1–16.** What parallels do you see between the disciples' response to Jesus' calming of the storm in Matthew 8:23–27 and the response of those aboard the ship bound for Tarshish once Jonah was thrown overboard? (Hint: Jonah 1:16)

✤ Personal Challenge

Over the course of the next week, start (or, if you already own one, continue) recording your prayer requests in a journal. Make a list of the various storms you've faced in the past, as well as storms you're facing in the present, and any hunches about those you may face in the future. Spend time asking for Jesus' presence, power, and protection in the midst of each and every storm.

8. Reflecting on past storms you've experienced, describe a time when God calmed a storm in a single moment. How does reflecting on that moment strengthen your faith and hope?

No matter what stormy situation you're facing, you can be encouraged that no difficulty is more powerful than God.

Digging Deeper

Read **Mark 4:37–41** and **Luke 8:22–25.** What details are included in these two accounts of Jesus calming the storm that aren't included in Matthew 8:23–27? Which of these details are meaningful to you right now? Explain.

There are three stages in the work of God:
Impossible; Difficult; Done.

James Hudson Taylor,
Christian missionary to China

When You're Between a Rock and a Hard Place

Tax Time

A man steps out from the crowd and begs Jesus to have compassion and heal his son, explaining that his son suffers from terrible seizures. Unlike ordinary seizures, these are caused by evil spirits. In the middle of such seizures, the son has been known to throw his body into fire or water.

The father tells Jesus he has already taken his beloved son to Jesus' followers for healing, but they couldn't help. "Bring him here to Me," Jesus responds (Matthew 17:17). In an instant, Jesus sends the evil spirits away and the boy is healed.

Later, when the disciples are alone with Jesus, one big question bubbles up inside of them: Why couldn't they help the boy? They tried everything they knew. Jesus shares with them the secret ingredient: faith.

Soon after the boy's healing, the disciples and Jesus travel into Capernaum, a small fishing village along the shore of the Sea of Galilee. The dust barely begins to settle from their entry into the city when tax collectors approach Peter outside a house.

The tax collectors ask Peter whether or not Jesus pays the required temple tax. Every adult male is supposed to pay an annual fee of two drachma, or two days of a skilled worker's pay, for the upkeep of the temple. (The drachma is a Greek coin used throughout history, which has only recently been replaced by the euro.) One can imagine the tax collectors are not as concerned with the money as they are with finding fault in Jesus. Peter doesn't hesitate to defend Jesus.

Peter and the tax collectors enter the house, but before Peter can explain who the visitors are, Jesus speaks first—He already knows what Peter needs. Jesus petitions him to go fishing and toss his line into the water. Peter obeys and, miraculously, finds a coin inside the first fish's mouth that will be enough for both his and Jesus' tax bill.

Both the stories of the son's healing and the coin in the fish's mouth emphasize the importance of faith and trust in Jesus. The disciples are reminded that faith—even the size of a mustard seed—is foundational in following Jesus. Peter discovers that he not only needs faith, he needs to act on that faith by following Jesus' instructions. Money doesn't fall from the sky into his open and empty purse. Effort is required.

God knows our needs. He knows the spaces where we are caught between a rock and a hard place—even before we offer the first words. No matter what situation is before us, we can trust that Jesus goes before us.

The disciples had been on quite a journey with Jesus—especially Peter, James, and John. In the beginning of Matthew 17, they experienced an

> Faith—even the size of a mustard seed—is foundational in following Jesus.

incredible moment when Jesus was transfigured before them. Then the disciples watched as Jesus set a boy free from evil spirits.

Despite being with Jesus for several years in full-time ministry—traveling, eating, and living with Jesus as He journeyed—the disciples were still learning and being challenged in their faith.

1. How have you seen your experience in getting to know God as an ongoing journey of learning and growing?

2. Read **Matthew 17:1–23**. How do you think the disciples' experiences described in these passages strengthened their faith?

After the transfiguration and healing of the boy with an evil spirit, one of the disciples faced a new challenge. The story of the temple tax is recorded only in the Gospel of Matthew, possibly because the encounter was of particular interest to Matthew—a former tax collector himself, the difference being that Matthew served as a tax collector for the Romans and these tax collectors served Jewish religious leaders.

In the story, a tax collector approached Peter and presented him with a question: Did Jesus pay the two-drachma tax? Peter answered without hesitation: Yes! Peter may have seen Jesus pay the tax before or he may have simply known that Jesus always met His obligations.

3. Read **Matthew 17:24–27**. When have you experienced God speaking or moving in your life before you realized the need you were facing?

The temple tax the collectors asked about in verse 24 originated in Exodus 30:11–16. Each Israelite age twenty and above was required to pay an offering to the Lord to be used for the service of the tent of meeting, or tabernacle. In Jesus' time, the tax was required for the service of the temple.

When heading back into the house, Jesus knew exactly what was on Peter's mind.

4. What two questions did Jesus ask Peter? (Hint: Matthew 17:25) Why do you think Jesus asked Peter what he thought? How was Peter's answer a revelation or moment of insight?

Throughout Scripture, whenever God asks someone a question, He already knows the answer. Yet, He often asks questions anyway so that we have the opportunity to consider the matter, reflect, think, and grow.

5. Look up the following passages and fill out the chart below. You may need to read a few verses before or after to gain the context to fill in each blank. In each of the passages, how did God's question change the person's understanding of the situation and/or him- or herself?

Passage	Who God Asked	What God Asked
Genesis 3:1–10		
Genesis 4:1–8		
Genesis 18:1–15		
Exodus 4:1–5		

Jesus instructed Peter to go fishing. This wasn't the first time Peter witnessed a miracle involving his profession. When Jesus first met Peter, He asked him to cast his nets on the other side of the boat, which nearly broke from all the fish brought in (see chapter seven). But this miracle didn't involve catching fish with nets; it involved only a single hook. Jesus told Peter to take the first fish he caught and open its mouth, and he would find the money he needed to pay the tax for both of them. It's significant that Jesus did this, when He could have simply pulled a miraculous coin from His satchel.

6. Why do you think some effort was demanded of Peter for the miraculous provision? In what ways have you seen God require some effort of you in order to experience miraculous provision in your own life?

7. When you pray for God to do something miraculous, to do what seems impossible, do you tend to think God will do it apart from your active participation? Or do you tend to believe He will involve you? Explain.

✢ Personal Challenge

Spend some time prayerfully asking God to meet the needs in your own life. Then spend some time prayerfully asking God to meet the needs in the lives of people you know. Consider practical ways God may be asking you to meet their needs, and accomplish one of them this week.

8. What do you sense God is calling you to do to help meet a specific need in either your own life or someone else's?

God is not
only with you but goes
before you in whatever
situation you're facing. You can
trust Jesus with your needs
and know He hears you.

Digging Deeper

Read **Psalm 31:23**. How does humility make you more able to receive from God? When have you found your pride getting in the way of what God wants to do in your life? How have you experienced God preserving you? Spend some time thanking God for His faithfulness in the past.

My spirit has become dry because it forgets
to feed on You.

St. John of the Cross,
Carmelite priest

When You're Physically and Spiritually Hungry

More Than Enough

Jesus and His twelve closest followers (known as disciples) hike up a mountain on the far side of the Sea of Galilee. John 6 describes a large crowd scrambling up the rocky ascent, hoping to experience a miracle. Jesus sits down and soon finds Himself surrounded by throngs of people hanging on His every word.

Looking out on the oncoming crowd, Jesus turns to one of His disciples, Philip, and asks where they will find bread to feed the multitude. Jesus already has a plan in mind, but He wants to deepen Philip's faith.

Philip runs the numbers in his head and realizes the cost to feed the five thousand men and countless other women and children would be more than half a year's wages. Even if they had the money, the amount they could buy still wouldn't be enough to satisfy everyone's hunger.

Andrew, another disciple, proposes a solution. He brings forward a boy offering his meal of five barley loaves and two fish. In light of the mass amount of people, the small portion seems insignificant. However, Jesus accepts the child's offering and requests that everyone take a seat. The masses sit down on the grass, eager to see what Jesus will do next.

One can imagine the seed of doubt in the disciples' hearts as they look at the loaves and fish. But Jesus doesn't hesitate. He takes the bread and gives thanks over the meal. Then Jesus begins to pass out the food to those seated. He does the same with the fish. The meal multiplies before the disciples' eyes.

When everyone has eaten until satisfied, Jesus asks His disciples to begin collecting the leftovers. Twelve baskets of bread remain. Excited by this miracle, the crowd attempts to make Jesus king by force. Before they can capture Him to crown Him, Jesus leaves.

The next day the crowd searches for Jesus, looking high and low. When they find Him, Jesus reflects on the miracle of the multiplying meal. He acknowledges they are not truly looking for Him but only want free food. He reminds them that once they eat bread, they will be hungry again in a matter of hours. But whoever comes to Jesus, the Bread of Life, will never go hungry again.

Distracted by physical hunger and the "wow factor" of the miracle, the crowd doesn't realize Jesus is concerned not just with their physical hunger but with their spiritual hunger.

> Once they eat bread, they will be hungry again in a matter of hours. But whoever comes to Jesus, the Bread of Life, will never go hungry again.

Sometimes when we find ourselves in the middle of a great need, we can become so focused on what we need, we miss the fact that God wants to give us the greatest gift of all—Himself! No matter what physical needs you're facing, rest assured that God wants to meet your need and provide an abundance of His presence.

The feeding of the five thousand is the only miracle recorded in all four of the gospels—Matthew, Mark, Luke, and John. The story retold in the above section is from John's point of view found in John 6.

Those who listened to Jesus all day were physically and spiritually hungry, and Jesus met their needs with abundance.

1. In the last year, when have you experienced Jesus sustaining you spiritually? Describe.

Throughout Scripture, God frequently provided for His people with an abundance of miraculous food. The Israelites fed on manna during their wanderings in the desert in Exodus 16. The Lord also provided Elisha with enough bread for his one hundred hungry men in 2 Kings 4:42–44. And a story of Jesus multiplying bread and fish for a crowd of four thousand is recorded in Mark 8:1–10.

2. God often meets our spiritual needs with spiritual food. When you're spiritually hungry for God, which disciplines or spiritual practices do you find most nourishing to your spirit? Place a check by them.

_____ Studying the Scripture   _____ Prayer

_____ Listening to a sermon or Bible teaching   _____ Fellowship

_____ Worship   _____ Silence/Solitude

_____ Giving   _____ Service

_____ Fasting   _____ Gratitude

_____ Confession   _____ Other

3. What prevents you from engaging in the spiritual practices you checked above with more consistency? How can you be more intentional about practicing them?

Because the feeding of the five thousand is primarily a miracle about food, we automatically think about the people's hunger, but we must remember they were tired, too. The disciples were likely exhausted from long hours of ministry. The crowds were exhausted from their long trek. Hunger coupled with exhaustion is challenging for any person. Being exhausted, hungry, and stressed can make a person want to withdraw from others.

4. Read **John 6:1–9**. How did Philip and Andrew respond to Jesus' question? Which character are you more like: Philip? Andrew? The boy? The crowd? Why?

Considering that feeding five thousand people would cost more than half a year's wages, the disciples' response was practical. But God's response to our needs isn't always practical. In other words, God's ways are often more generous and abundant than our own.

5. Read **John 6:10–15**. How has God been using you as an instrument to care or provide for others in this season of your life?

John 6:11 uses three verbs to describe what Jesus did. He *took* the loaves, and after He *had given* thanks, He *distributed* the food. Forms of these three verbs are found in other Gospel accounts of the feeding of the multitude (Matthew 14:13–21; Mark 6:31–44; Luke 9:10–17), as well as during the conversation at the Last Supper (Matthew 26:17–30; Mark 14:12–26; Luke 22:7–39; John 13:1—17:26).

After giving thanks, Jesus passed the bread and fish to the crowds. Everyone ate until they were satisfied. Then they picked up the leftovers so nothing went to waste. The miracle wasn't only in the provision but in the abundance.

6. How have you experienced God providing lavishly to a need or as a blessing in your life? How did this experience impact your faith?

Jesus knew there were some in the crowd who chose to follow Him only to solve their short-term problems—like hunger. But Jesus also knew that in the crowd were those who would understand the miracle as feeding something deeper than the physical—the spiritual. Later in John 6, Jesus used the miracle of multiplying the loaves to reveal His identity as the Son of God and long-awaited Messiah.

7. Read **John 6:25–40**. Why do you think the Jews had such a hard time recognizing Jesus as the Bread of Life? In what ways do you struggle to recognize Jesus as your sustenance in life?

✣ Personal Challenge

Spend some time looking up the various mentions of bread in the Bible. Consider using a website like biblegateway.com to do a word search for the word *bread*, and explore the various mentions, uses, and references to bread in the Bible. Make a list of the ways God is your provider. Over the next week, thank God each day for providing in all the ways He has for you.

Jesus offered life-giving bread from heaven to the crowd. The bread Jesus mentioned wasn't the physical bread given to the multitude, or the bread that rained down from heaven under Moses' leadership, recorded in Exodus 16. Jesus identified Himself as the Bread of Life. It's also worth noting that Bethlehem, the name of the city in which Jesus was born, means "the city of bread."

Though the resources we have may be limited or inadequate, God still invites us to entrust what we have to Him. God can bless and multiply even the smallest of offerings—to meet not only our own needs but countless needs of those around us.

8. In what area of your life are you most likely to disqualify yourself from giving or becoming involved because what you feel you have to offer—in time, gifts, or talents—seems inadequate? What steps can you take in the next week to begin offering your time, talents, and gifts wholly to God?

Sometimes
when we find ourselves
in the middle of a great need, we
can become so focused on what we need,
we miss the fact that God wants to give us
the greatest gift of all—Himself! Whatever
brokenness you're experiencing, rest
assured God wants to give you an
abundance of His presence.

Digging Deeper

Read **Exodus 16**. What parallels do you see between the ways God met the Israelites' needs in the desert and the ways Jesus met the needs of the multitudes? In what ways have you experienced Jesus as the Bread of Life in your own life? How has your faith been nourished and satisfied by this spiritual bread?

> The One who goes ahead of you, opening up the way, is the same One who stays close and never lets go of your hand.

Sarah Young,
Author of *Jesus Calling*

When You've Lost Your Most Precious

A Widow's Son

Continuing on His journey of ministering and performing miracles, Jesus journeys to Nain, a town located near the Sea of Galilee. A large crowd and the disciples follow, eager to see what Jesus will do next.

Luke 7:11–17 tells how as Jesus draws closer to the town's gate, He notices a funeral procession. A young man has died—the only remaining family of a widow. Members of the community accompany the widow to support her in her grief.

The widow's son is most likely carried out on a funeral bier, a pallet that was essentially a first-century hearse. His body is wrapped in linens and anointed with spices out of respect. One can only imagine the grief and pain the widowed mother's face displays.

When Jesus sees her, He feels compassion toward the woman. Not only has this woman experienced the loss of a son but her future is bleak: she likely faces poverty without any male in the family to provide for her.

Jesus approaches the funeral procession and encourages the widow not to cry—both an echo of something Jesus declared earlier in His ministry and a foreshadowing of what was to come: your weeping will turn to laughter (see Luke 6:21). Jesus stretches out His hand to touch the bier where the dead son is lying. Everything seems to pause as the men carrying the body stop walking. The onlookers watch with anticipation as Jesus begins to transform the mother's life forever.

Against all odds, the corpse takes a breath and sits up. The young man is alive!

Jesus commands the young man to get up.

Against all odds, the corpse takes a breath and sits up. The young man is alive! He begins speaking. One can only envision the joy that fills the mother's heart as Jesus presents the son to her. Jesus walks into the widow's unspeakable pain and offers hope and new life.

Everyone is filled with awe and wonder at the miracle. The community cannot contain the good news. With joy and glee, they begin praising God, thanking Him for the young man's new life. Word of Jesus soon spreads throughout the countryside. The people believe that God has come to help His people. Family is restored. Pain is turned to joy. What was lost is now found.

During our moments of greatest need, we often face the temptation to give up hope, especially when we have lost the things most precious to us. But, as happened to the widow in this story, Jesus' heart reaches out to us. God will not leave us alone in our pain, but instead shows compassion. He enters into our lives, restores hope, and offers us new life.

The biblical city of Nain is considered to be modern-day Nein, about six miles from Nazareth. As Jesus and His followers reached the city's gate and viewed the funeral procession, professional mourners were probably in the mix. Jewish tradition said that even the poorest in Israel should hire professional wailers and flute players.

In ancient Israel, widows were dependent on their male children to support them, as ancient societies didn't provide any governmental relief for the poor. This placed the widow in the story in a precarious situation. Not only did she face the loneliness and isolation of losing her precious family members, she also faced losing her means of support.

1. Read **Luke 7:11–15**. What did Jesus say to the woman? (Hint: Luke 7:13) What does this story reveal about God's attitude toward us in times of pain, loss, and need?

2. How does cultivating compassion impact your prayer life? Personal relationships? Readiness to serve others?

For the first time in the Gospel of Luke, Jesus is referred to as "Lord" in Luke 5:8. Jesus was revealed not just as a good man, a wise teacher, or a great prophet but as the Lord, with the power to turn weeping into joy. To perform this miracle, Jesus reached out and touched the body. This minor detail is highly significant. Old Testament law prohibited the touching of dead bodies or coffins, because the action rendered a person ceremonially unclean.

3. What risks have you taken to help someone in need?

When Jesus stretched out His hand and touched the open coffin, He commanded the son to get up. With only a few words from Jesus, the boy was alive and began to speak. The crowd looked on with awestruck disbelief as they began to process the miracle.

4. Read **Luke 7:16, 17**. What was the response of those who saw the miracle of the son coming back to life?

The people proclaimed in verse 16 that "God [had] visited His people." A similar phrase is also used in Ruth 1:6 and 1 Samuel 2:21 as a blessing.

5. When in the last month have you sensed God speaking a word of life, hope, or restoration to you through the Scriptures? How did that word change your perspective or attitude?

6. Look up each of the following passages. What does each scripture reveal about the power of hope in our lives?

Scripture:	Power of Hope:
1 John 3:3	
Psalm 31:24	
Psalm 42:11	
Psalm 71:5	

7. Reflecting on the chart above, which of the passages is most meaningful to you?

✤ Personal Challenge

Ask God to what areas of your life He wants to bring life, restoration, and healing. Pay attention to those areas and ask God to arise in you. Then throughout the upcoming week write down wherever you see God rising in your life. Share your notes with the group the next time you gather.

8. In what area of your life—including the broken places—do you sense the Holy Spirit saying to you, "Arise!"

As Jesus walked
into the widow's moment of
great pain and loss, He also wants
to walk into our moments of pain
and loss with the intention of
offering hope and life.

Digging Deeper

Read **1 Kings 17:17–24** about Elijah's encounter with the widow at Zarephath. How does this story compare and contrast to the story of the widow at Nain? In what ways does Jesus' healing of the widow at Nain demonstrate He is more than a prophet but the Son of God? How are you encouraged to know that Jesus has authority over death?

Those who keep speaking about the sun while
walking under a cloudy sky are messengers
of hope, the true saints of our day.

Henri J. Nouwen,
Catholic priest and author

When All Hope Is Lost

Lazarus

Sometime after restoring sight to a blind man, Jesus receives
devastating news. One of His beloved friends, Lazarus, is very
ill and will likely die. Instead of traveling directly to Bethany, the
home of Lazarus, Jesus waits two days. He offers the mysterious
assurance that Lazarus will not die.

But by the time Jesus arrives in Bethany, Lazarus has already
been buried for four days and Mary and Martha, Lazarus's sisters,
are grieving the death of their brother.

When Martha hears of Jesus' arrival, she runs out to greet
Him. She laments that if Jesus had been there, Lazarus would not
have died. But Jesus assures Martha that Lazarus will rise from
the dead.

Then Jesus makes one of the most amazing proclamations
in all of Scripture: "I am the resurrection and the life. He who

believes in Me, though he may die, he shall live. And whoever lives and believes in Me shall never die" (John 11:25, 26).

When Mary sees Jesus, she tosses aside any pretense and flings herself at His feet, crying out, like Martha, that His presence would have prevented her brother's death.

Compassion pours out of Jesus as He weeps alongside Mary and the other mourners. Arriving at Lazarus's tomb, Jesus is again moved with emotion and requests that the stone covering the entrance to the tomb be removed.

Martha protests that rolling away the stone will unleash a nasty smell. With patience and gentleness, Jesus reminds Martha that if she believes, she will see God's glory. Then Jesus lifts His eyes toward heaven and thanks God for hearing His prayers. He prays out loud so those watching may believe God sent Him.

Taking a deep breath, Jesus calls Lazarus out of the tomb. Still wrapped in burial clothing, Lazarus waddles outside in response. Jesus tells the crowd outside to help unwrap Lazarus and set him free.

Lazarus is alive!

The miracle proves once again that Jesus is who He says He is—the Son of God. But the wonder of this story isn't limited to Lazarus coming back to life; there is also much to learn from the way in which Jesus responded to Lazarus's death. Jesus mourned with those who mourned. What an incredible reminder! When we experience betrayal, loss, and death, Jesus mourns with us. We can call out to Him with confidence that He hears us and understands.

> "I am the resurrection and the life. He who believes in Me, though he may die, he shall live. And whoever lives and believes in Me shall never die"
> (John 11:25, 26).

The Hebrew name for Lazarus is Eleazer, which can be translated "God helps" or "God is helper." Sometimes people confuse the Lazarus Jesus encounters here with a different Lazarus. Two stories about a man named Lazarus are mentioned in the Gospels—in John 11 and Luke 16:19–31. Scholars debate whether or not both accounts describe the same man, but many conclude the poor beggar described in the Luke passage is a different Lazarus. They note that the Lazarus of Luke is highly unlikely to have had the resources Mary, Martha, and Lazarus had to host Jesus and His disciples on several occasions.

In this story, we see God healing when all hope is lost.

1. Read **John 11:1–5**. How would you describe the relationship Lazarus, Mary, and Martha had with Jesus?

When Jesus heard of Lazarus's condition, He didn't travel to the city of Bethany right away—much to the confusion of His followers. Instead, He waited until His friend had been buried for four days.

2. Read **John 11:6–19**. Why do you think Jesus didn't respond immediately to the news of Lazarus's sickness? (Hint: John 11:4) When in the last year have you been frustrated by God's seemingly slow response to a situation?

Likely frustrated by Jesus' tardy arrival, Martha voiced her confusion and heartache to Jesus. He challenged her understanding of who He was, but Martha remained confused.

3. Read **John 11:19–27**. How did Jesus challenge Martha's faith and understanding of Him in this passage?

John 11:25 records the fifth of the seven "I am" statements in John's gospel: "I am the bread of life" (John 6:35); "I am the light of the world" (John 8:12); "I am the door" (John 10:9); "I am the good shepherd" (John 10:11); "I am the resurrection and the life" (John 11:25); "I am the way, the truth, and the life" (John 14:6); "I am the vine" (John 15:5). The emphatic Greek *ego emi* is reminiscent of the name God offers to Moses in Exodus 3:14, "I AM." These statements declare the identity of Jesus.

Martha claimed to understand that Lazarus would rise again on the last day. This was standard teaching in Jewish traditions, based off of Daniel 12:2, which says, "Many of those who sleep in the dust of the earth shall awake, some to everlasting life, some to shame and everlasting contempt."

4. How have you discovered Jesus' claim in John 11:25, 26 to be true in your life? How does Jesus' statement affect your understanding of life and death?

John 11:35 offers the shortest verse in the Bible: "Jesus wept." Only two other places in the New Testament record Jesus crying. He wept over Jerusalem as He approached the city for the last time in Luke 19:41. And Hebrews 5:7 tells us Jesus offered up prayers to God with cries and tears.

5. Read **John 11:28–36**. Why do you think Jesus wept even though He knew what He was going to do? What does Jesus' weeping reveal about His response to our own moments of pain and loss (John 11:33–35)?

After being filled with emotion toward His friends, Jesus asked that the stone covering Lazarus's tomb be removed. This request was met with dissention and confusion.

6. Read **John 11:37–44**. Do you think the protests by the onlookers and Martha were valid concerns? Why or why not? How do you tend to respond to impossible situations?

Jesus gazed upward during His prayer. Whereas Christians often pray with their eyes closed to avoid distractions, Jewish people pray with their eyes open. Neither is specified in Scripture as the correct approach.

7. Look up the following passages. What does each one reveal about God's power over death? Place a star by the passage that is most meaningful to you.

Psalm 49:15:

John 5:21:

John 5:25:

John 6:40:

John 11:25:

Acts 26:8:

2 Corinthians 1:9:

2 Corinthians 4:14:

✤ Personal Challenge

Take a moment to think about your default reaction
to impossible situations. Ask God to show you how
He might want you to adjust your initial response
in those kinds of situations. What sorts of situations
do you anticipate encountering this week that might
challenge your commitment to trust God?

8. Whom do you know that needs compassion and someone to mourn
alongside? How can you show compassion to others who are suffering?

When we
experience betrayal, loss,
and death, Jesus mourns with us.
We need not fear death, because
Jesus is the resurrection
and the life.

Digging Deeper

Read **Psalm 103:13** and **Hebrews 4:15**. What comfort do you find in knowing that God has sympathy and compassion for you in your time of need? When have you been through a difficult time that expanded your compassion for others?

Through the window of my brokenness I
see the face of God. I used to only see my
own reflection in the glass, what was wrong,
unlovely, and weak. But when God in His
fierce and fiery love allowed the walls of my
glass cage to smash and splinter . . . I saw Him.

Sheila Walsh,
Women of Faith speaker and author

When Everyone Turns Their Back on You

The Man Born Blind

As Jesus and His disciples stroll down a road, a begging
man who was born blind catches their eye. Tugging on Jesus'
clothes like curious children, the disciples ask Him what sin caused
the man's blindness. They assume, like others in their day, that
physical imperfections are caused by a sin committed by the
person or his parents.

Jesus challenges this cultural understanding. His reply shocks
them: no one sinned; instead, God's glory will be shown through
this blind man.

He reminds the disciples of something He told them earlier: "I am the light of the world" (John 8:12). With that, Jesus hawks some spit into the dirt and swirls the saliva around. Jesus takes the mud and smears the concoction over the blind man's eyes. While this may seem like a strange spa facial, Jesus has something greater in mind.

Jesus encourages the blind man to wash his eyes in the Pool of Siloam, a source of water found outside of the city wall. What happens next is not because of magical qualities in the water, but because of Jesus.

The man dips his hands into the cool water and scrubs the mud off his eyes. As soon as he finishes, he opens his eyes. He has to squint quickly because light pours into the darkness. Vibrant colors and shapes come into focus.

He can see!

"I am the light of the world" (John 8:12).

The Light of the World has brought brightness and life to a man blind from birth.

The man walks home and astounds his friends and family. Even his closest friends don't believe this new man is actually the same person. No one can believe the miraculous act that has taken place.

The man's neighbors bring him before the Pharisees, the religious authorities of the ancient Jews. Everyone's curious as to how he gained his vision. Questions are launched toward the man. How did this happen? Who is this Jesus?

Instead of celebrating his sight, his friends and authorities attempt to dispel the miracle. He tells them what he knows: "I was blind. A man rubbed some mud on my eyes, I washed, and now I can see."

After hearing the man's story, the Pharisees banish him from the temple. He is shut out from the community he knows and loves. Instead of rejoicing in the miracle with him, they shun him.

Jesus hears of this and searches for the man. Now completely healed, both physically and spiritually, the man begins to worship Jesus.

Jesus restored not only the man's physical sight but his spiritual sight as well. In the same way, Jesus longs to bring more than physical healing to our lives. He desires to wrap His healing arms around every area of our lives—no matter what difficulty we're facing.

The disciples followed Jesus and watched as He performed signs and miracles beyond their wildest imaginations. But when they approached one blind man in desperate need of a miracle, the disciples didn't expect Jesus to act. Instead of extending compassion and advocating on his behalf, they assumed the blind man was deserving of his ailment. Jewish culture associated sin and suffering, but Jesus broke through that stigma in John 9.

1. Read **John 9:1–5**. The disciples didn't ask Jesus to heal the man because they thought he was blind as a result of his (or his parents') sin. When have you been more concerned with a theological issue than doing the work of God?

When the disciples asked Jesus what the man had done to cause his own blindness, Jesus' answer shocked them: "Neither this man nor his parents sinned, but that the works of God should be revealed in him" (John 9:3). Verse 3 contains the Greek word *hina*, a clause that indicates the result of an action or situation and that can sometimes denote a purpose. The word usually translates "so that" or "in order that." The clause as it is used here signifies that even evil contributes to God's glory.

2. Which aspect of Jesus' answer may have been most surprising to the disciples? What aspect is most surprising to you? Why?

Suffering from blindness was widespread in ancient times. Unclean water, leprosy, and infection led to this rampant disorder. Jesus continually referred to the blind in His parables and metaphors, since His audience was familiar with the nearly impossible-to-cure disorder.

3. Read **John 9:6, 7**. What did Jesus ask of the blind man? What did the blind man's obedience reveal about his faith?

Jesus spit in the dirt, mixed the mud, and wiped the creation on the blind man's eyes. The pagan god of medicine, Asclepius, also was famed for healing with magical saliva. Jesus was possibly displaying His authority over the pagan gods of the time when He restored the man-born-blind's sight.

4. Read **John 9:8–12**. What was the initial response to the blind man's healing? Why do you think there were so many different responses to the healing?

The blind man who until then had been found begging around town was now claiming to have had his sight completely restored by a man named Jesus. His neighbors, onlookers, the Pharisees, and even his parents had a hard time believing this was true.

5. Read **John 9:13–17**. Have you ever been caught up in a religious controversy? What was the most difficult aspect of the experience?

6. Read **John 9:18–23**. How do you think the blind man felt about his parents' response to his healing?

After confronting the man-born-blind's parents, the Pharisees returned to question the healed man. They demanded an explanation as to how he was healed. The man-born-blind tried to tell the religious leaders that his healing could only come from one source: God.

7. Read **John 9:24–41**. What encouragement do you find in knowing Jesus pursued the formerly blind man when he was kicked out of the temple? When have you experienced God comforting you when everyone seemed to turn his or her back on you?

✣ Personal Challenge

Spend some time this week investing in the people
from question 8 whom you recognized as isolated or
alone. Write them a card and stick the note in the mail.
Invite them to lunch with a group of friends. Ask how
you can pray for them. Become a source of comfort
and encouragement for these people in your life.

John 9 expresses the progression of understanding the character and identity of Jesus throughout the story. John 9:11 states His name, "Jesus." John 9:17 declares Jesus is a prophet. John 9:22 explains Jesus is the Christ. Finally, in John 9:33 Jesus is described as being from God. While the Pharisees never saw this progression, the man-born-blind did, and believed.

8. Is someone you know feeling isolated and alone? Who? How can you be a source of encouragement and comfort to him or her this week?

Jesus longs to
bring more than physical
healing to our lives; He wants
to bring healing to every aspect
of our lives, no matter what
challenges we're facing.

Digging Deeper

Read **Mark 8:22–26, Matthew 9:27–31**, and **Matthew 20:29–34**. Take note of any details that stand out to you as you read these stories of people whom Jesus healed from blindness. Then read **Luke 4:18**, which is based on Isaiah 61:1. How was Jesus fulfilling this proclamation and revealing He was the Messiah through these healings?

God Brings Healing Through Our Broken Places

God not only meets us in the broken places and brings healing, but He often uses our experiences to draw us outward and bring encouragement and hope to others.

> Never be afraid to trust an unknown future to a known God.

Corrie ten Boom,
author and Holocaust survivor

When You're at the End of Your Rope

A Huge Catch of Fish

Surrounded by crowds, Jesus walks along the shore of a great lake when He sees some fishermen washing their nets in the distance. They've been up all night casting their nets and bringing them in, only to find that all of their hard work hasn't produced a single fish. Exhausted from the long hours, they rinse the seaweed and scum from their nets before heading home.

The fishermen—James, John, and Simon Peter—likely notice the large crowd on the shore of the lake. Men, women, and children surround the man who is talking. As they wash their nets, the man and crowd move toward them until the man steps into one of the boats and makes an unusual request: put the boat out a small distance from the shore.

Simon Peter agrees and sits aboard the boat as Jesus begins teaching the large crowd. Scripture doesn't record what Jesus says, but one can imagine the words are thought-provoking, compelling, and like nothing Simon Peter or the other fishermen have ever heard before.

When Jesus finishes teaching, He turns to Simon Peter with a second unusual request. Jesus asks Simon Peter to go to the deeper water and put down the nets for a catch.

Something about Jesus' teaching must have penetrated Simon Peter's heart. Simon Peter recognizes Jesus as more than an ordinary person, but someone of authority: "Master," he calls Him (Luke 5:5). But Simon explains the situation to Jesus: as fishermen, they have worked all night without a single catch. They are at the end of their rope—ready to head home empty-handed. Though the odds are improbable, Simon does as Jesus instructs, and he lowers the nets.

Whenever we find ourselves at the end of our rope in life—because of a need or personal failure—Christ meets us.

Before the nets surface, the flapping of fish is seen and heard by everyone in the boat. Wide-eyed with awe and excitement, Simon Peter doesn't help bring in the catch. Instead, his first reaction is to drop to his knees and declare his own sinful, imperfect nature. He recognizes Jesus as Lord. The astonishment of Simon Peter quickly spreads to the other fishermen, and they're awed by the great catch. Jesus assures them the fish in the nets are only a foretaste of what's to come. Though they catch fish today, they'll spend their lives capturing people's hearts and introducing them to Christ (Luke 5:10).

Responding to the invitation to become disciples, these men spend the next few years listening to Jesus' teaching, witnessing Him perform miracles, and watching the way He challenges the religious establishment of the time until His crucifixion and death. And in an interesting parallel, after His death and resurrection Jesus appears to His disciples in a way reminiscent of His initial meeting with them.

Again, Simon Peter and some of the disciples have spent a night on the water and caught nothing. John 21 records that, as the dawn approaches, a man on the shore instructs them to place their nets on the other side of the boat. They obey, and again, the nets are bursting with fish. The miracle comes at a crucial time for Simon Peter. After Jesus' arrest, Simon Peter had denied Jesus three times and probably wondered if he still had a plan and purpose as a disciple. In the wake of a miracle that reminds Simon Peter of his original calling as a disciple, Jesus reminds him that indeed, he does have a profound purpose: to follow Christ with reckless abandon.

These stories remind us that whenever we find ourselves at the end of our rope in life—because of a need or personal failure—Christ meets us. Not only does Christ provide for us in surprising and unexpected ways in such moments, but He calls us to greater discipleship and obedience so that we will become a blessing to others.

The Gospel of Luke identifies the shores of the lake that Jesus stood on as Gennesaret, but this body of water is better known as the Sea of Galilee. Luke's gospel always refers to Galilee as a lake, whereas the other gospel writers call it a sea.

After fishing all night, Simon Peter, James, and John were empty-handed. They hadn't caught a single fish.

1. Read **Luke 5:1–7**. Describe a time in the past week when you felt at the end of your rope and frustrated by a lack of provision or productivity.

It's worth noting that the disciples were washing the nets during the day since the nets were used only for night fishing. This detail underscores the miracle of the catch: during the day, fish could see and would avoid the nets.

2. How did Simon Peter and the other disciples respond to Jesus' instruction to place their nets on the other side of the boat? (Hint: Luke 5:5)

An obvious shift occurred in Simon Peter's character in Luke 5:8, when Luke first used the compound name Simon Peter. Before then, he had always referred to the disciple as Simon. From verse 8 to the end of the gospel, Luke continued to call him Peter (the only exception being when he was quoting another person saying "Simon Peter").

3. Read **Luke 5:8–11**. What were Simon Peter and the other disciples' responses to the great catch of fish? How do you tend to respond when you find yourself in the powerful presence of God?

When the fishermen arrived on shore, they left everything—probably the greatest catch of their lives—in order to follow Christ. They became disciples. Jesus met these fishermen when they were at the end of their rope—and called them to become disciples in the fullest sense. Their response would impact not only their lives but the lives of countless others.

4. When you're at the end of your rope, do you tend to think of God meeting your personal needs only in the moment or do you tend to look at the situation as an opportunity for God to meet you and call you to greater discipleship and obedience? Explain.

After becoming disciples of Jesus and experiencing His teaching and miracles, the disciples witnessed His brutal death. After His resurrection, Jesus reappeared to the disciples in a similar fashion as that described in Luke's gospel—but surprisingly, the disciples didn't recognize Him at first.

5. Read **John 21:1–11**. What are the similarities and differences between this account and how Jesus appeared to the disciples in Luke 5:1–11? Does it surprise you that the disciples didn't recognize Jesus on the shore? Why or why not?

The discussion between Jesus and Peter in John 21 occurred after a miraculous catch of fish, a reminder of when Peter was first called to become a disciple. Jesus restored Peter after he denied Christ three times, and His question to Peter about love ("Do you love Me?"), repeated three times, paralleled Peter's three denials. The charcoal fire was reminiscent of the smoky fire on the night of Peter's betrayal.

6. Read **John 21:12–25**. Why do you think Jesus went to such great lengths to restore Peter—a man who probably felt he was at the end of his rope after denying Christ three times (John 18:15–27)? What does this reveal about Jesus' tremendous love for His disciples—including us?

After Jesus' death, Peter and the other disciples returned to their day job—fishing. Rather than following the God-calling on their lives, they self-determined what they should do. In light of this, they caught nothing. However, when Jesus directed their actions, they caught a netful.

7. Following this miraculous catch of fish, how did Jesus again call Peter and the disciples to a discipleship that would not only impact their lives but the lives of countless others? (Hint: John 21:15–17)

✤ Personal Challenge

Spend some time prayerfully considering to whom Jesus is calling you to reach out to share your faith as a fisherwoman. Look for opportunities to spend time with that person—possibly on a walk or over a meal—over the course of the next week, and talk about the work Jesus is doing in your own life.

Jesus asked Peter three different times if he loved Him. The Greek language contains three words for "love." Two of those are seen in John 21:15–17. *Agape* is a self-sacrificing, unconditional, Christlike love. *Phileo* is a love between friends or brothers. Jesus asked Peter if he loved Him with *agape*, but Peter responded that he loved Jesus with *phileo*. This went on for two of the three questions. Finally, in the last question, Jesus asked Peter if he loved Him with *phileo*. Peter replied that he did love Jesus with *phileo*. Scholars are torn as to why the two forms of love are used. The variety is possibly used to show Peter's repeated declaration of love for Christ, as Christ passed along His role of shepherd to Peter, instructing him to "feed [His] sheep" (v. 17).

Sometimes we can be tempted to think that when God meets us at the end of our rope it's all about us—but often God uses these moments of His miraculous provision to call us to greater discipleship and obedience, and to become a blessing and source of encouragement for others.

8. What situations in your own life are opportunities for greater discipleship and obedience to Jesus, as well as opportunities to become a blessing to others?

When you feel
like you're at the end of your
rope, God will meet you there—
sometimes in the most surprising ways.
Such moments become opportunities for
greater discipleship and obedience, as
well as an opportunity to impact
the lives of others.

Digging Deeper

Read **Isaiah 6:1–7** and **Luke 5:1–11.** What parallels do you see between the way the prophet Isaiah responded to encountering God's presence and the way Peter responded to encountering God's presence following the catch? When have you been astonished and awed by God's presence in your life? When has an encounter with God exposed your own sinfulness and need for Him?

When thou hast truly thanked the Lord for
every blessing sent.
But little time will then remain for murmur or
lament.

Hannah More,
poet and playwright

When You Need Healing

Ten People with Leprosy

As Jesus enters a village on His way into Jerusalem, voices catch
His ear. A little distance away, ten men who have leprosy cry out
to Jesus. Their desperate pleas for mercy express their need to be
healed.

Believed to be highly contagious, these ten have been shut
out from their community—forced to live on the outskirts and to
alert anyone who comes near to stay away. A couple of the men
have permanent damage to their nerves and skin. Others have
irrevocable injuries to their eyes and other body parts.

Jesus sees the men in their brokenness and pours out
compassion on them. He requests something strange. The men
are to go and show themselves to the priests, the only religious
leaders who can declare the men "clean"—a recognition that would
allow the men to reintegrate into their families and community.

For these men, each step toward the priest is a step closer to possible rejection. But instead of questioning Jesus or delaying, the ten quickly turn and follow His instructions. Within moments their leprosy disappears. They watch the scabs and scars that plagued their bodies for years melt away.

The men likely sprint toward the priests now so they can see their families!

But after one man sees that he is healed, he sprints in the opposite direction—back to where they had just come from, back to Jesus, showering declarations of adoration along the way. He throws his body at Jesus' feet, praising God in a loud voice, thanking Him. Jesus has met the man in his brokenness and the man cannot contain his gratefulness.

He has healed ten men from their illness. And yet, only one has come back to praise God.

Jesus asks the healed man where the other nine are. He has healed ten men from their illness. And yet, only one has come back to praise God.

Jesus tells the man to stand up. Faith has healed him. With a miracle, Jesus heals ten men from a disease that has ruined their lives. Filled with gratitude, one man rushes back to Jesus and throws himself at His feet. Endless words and songs of praise escape his lips. He praises and thanks the One who met him in his brokenness and offered healing.

Just like the one man who turned back to thank Jesus, we too are called to live lives abounding with gratitude. With every chance we get, we can offer thanks to our Healer. Living a life of gratitude is not difficult but comes effortlessly when we take a moment to remember how God has worked in our lives. Whenever we experience God's healing in our lives, our response is to be like the one man with leprosy who turned back—full of thanks and praise!

Those diagnosed with leprosy were required by law to separate from society. They even had to warn oncoming people of their presence to avoid spreading their uncleanness to others. In Jewish culture, there was no difference between a person with leprosy and a corpse. These ten men probably banded together as a group of outcasts—even overlooking their social or religious differences.

1. Read **Luke 17:11–14**. What did the people with leprosy say as they cried out to Jesus? In what area of your life have you been crying out to Jesus?

Jesus instructed the men to show themselves to the priests. As they followed His instructions, they were cleansed. After being declared clean by the priest, the healed men were then required to offer sin offerings as thanks to God. Healing a person of leprosy meant both physical and social relief. The ten could return to their families and community as normal men.

Only priests had the authority to declare a person clean or unclean. Leviticus 13 and 14 provide instructions on how priests were to diagnose particular conditions. After seeing he was healed, one Samaritan man forgot about the priests and sprinted back to Jesus.

2. Read **Luke 17:15, 16**. What was unique about this person's response? Do you think his response was proportional to the gift of healing he received? Why or why not?

The Samaritan was the only man who returned to thank Jesus. In ancient culture, Samaritans were despised by the Jews. Samaritans were a mixed race of Jews and Babylonians. Both Jewish and Samaritan religious leaders taught against the other group. The Jewish men with leprosy felt no need (or forgot) to return to thank Jesus, but the Samaritan man recognized God's role in the healing. This is reminiscent of Luke 10:30–37 and the parable of the Good Samaritan.

3. When was the last time you were moved to worship God with passion?

Jesus responded to the Samaritan man's gratitude by asking three questions. Through these questions we see that Jesus expected gratitude from all ten of the men He healed. This relates to the parable He told earlier in Luke 17—God deserves proper thanks.

4. Read **Luke 17:17–19**. What three questions did Jesus ask in response to the healed man? What do you think Jesus was trying to emphasize?

While the remaining nine men still needed to show themselves to the priests and offer a sin offering in the temple, the one man who turned back to Jesus was healed by his faith.

Luke intentionally didn't reveal until verse 16 that the man who did what was good in Jesus' eyes was a Samaritan. When the Jews of that day read this verse, they probably gasped. In their minds, the Jews should have been the ones showing gratitude to the Messiah, not a hated Samaritan.

5. What types of situations or attitudes lead you toward ingratitude? What negative impact does ingratitude have on your life?

6. Look up the following passages. What does each passage reveal about the importance of gratitude?

Scripture	Importance of Gratitude
Psalm 100:1–5	
1 Chronicles 16:8–12	
Philippians 1:3–7	
1 Corinthians 4:7	
1 Thessalonians 5:18	
Hebrews 13:15	

7. In the space below, make a list of ten things you're grateful that Christ has done for you.

✢ Personal Challenge

Create an attitude of gratitude book. Create a list of 365 things or people in your life that you are thankful for. Write them down and bind them together at a local office supplies store. Spend time decorating the cover and each page with markers, feathers, jewels, or fun sheets of scrapbooking paper. Each day, spend time thanking God for that item on your list. Offer up your list as a prayer of gratitude to God.

8. What can you do to develop an attitude of gratitude in your life?

Whenever
Jesus meets us in
our brokenness, we have the
opportunity to express gratitude
through thanksgiving
and praise.

Digging Deeper

Read **Psalm 150**. Rewrite this Psalm in your own words. In what ways do thanksgiving and praise go hand in hand? In what areas of your life do you struggle to give God thanks and praise? Spend some time prayerfully considering how you can praise God even in the midst of difficult situations.

Faith is blind—except upward. It is blind to impossibilities, and deaf to doubt. It listens only to God and sees only His power and acts accordingly.

S. D. Gordon,
Christian author and speaker

When God Asks You to Step Out of the Boat

Walking on Water

Jesus finishes feeding thousands with a handful of bread and a few fish, and in the wake of this unforgettable miracle He sends His disciples to the other side of the Sea of Galilee. Once alone, Jesus heads up the side of a mountain to pray.

Later that night, a storm begins to brew. The disciples feel the spray of the waves on their tired bodies. They begin rowing toward shore for safety, but the wind and waves prevent them from making any progress.

The disciples notice a spooky figure off in the distance, coming toward them amidst the storm. Crying out in fear, the disciples aren't sure which is worse: a ghost approaching them or the storm threatening their lives.

A familiar voice calls out above the howling winds and crashing waves. The figure moving toward them claims to be Jesus! That would mean Jesus walked about three miles in the thick of the storm to the helpless boat.

Known throughout the Gospels for his speaking-before-thinking nature, Peter becomes the spokesperson for the other eleven disciples. The feisty disciple shouts with boldness that if it really is Jesus, then He should ask Peter to join Him for a stroll on the water.

Jesus replies with one loaded command: come.

Peter hoists himself onto the side of the wave-tossed boat. He swivels his feet toward Jesus and slowly stretches his toes downward. Keeping his eyes on Jesus, Peter defies nature and takes his first step on water. Peter carefully steps from crest to crest on his way toward the Master.

Something vies for Peter's attention in the corner of his eye. The storm! The wind is still howling and the waves are still crashing beneath him. Terrified, he takes his eyes from Jesus and immediately begins to sink.

Crying out to Jesus for help, Peter's wave-walking voyage quickly changes from awesome to awful. In response, Jesus reaches out His hand and lifts Peter to safety.

Carrying Peter back into the boat, Jesus calms the storm and reprimands Peter with gentleness for taking his eyes off of Him—displaying a small amount of faith.

Peter's bold request of Jesus leads to the adventure of a lifetime as recorded in Matthew 14. When Peter gets out of the boat and obeys Jesus,

When Peter gets out of the boat and obeys Jesus, things go as planned!

things go as planned! But as soon as he focuses on the situation around him, it quickly turns for the worse. Despite Peter's small amount of faith, Jesus immediately lifts Peter into the safety of His arms, reminding Peter who controls the wind and waves.

Sometimes the storms in life give us the opportunity to grow in our faith. Even when we begin to lose sight of our goal and become fearful, we can call out to Jesus. He is quick to rescue and draw us into His healing hands.

After a miraculous meal provision for five thousand, Jesus asked His disciples to go ahead of Him and begin to cross the Sea of Galilee. Jesus then ascended a nearby mountain to pray from dusk until around three in the morning. He took time to commune with His Father. This followed the Old Testament theme found in Exodus 34:31–34 and Psalm 121:1 of praying to God on the mountains.

1. Read **Matthew 14:22–24**. What role did prayer play in Jesus' life and ministry? How did prayer empower Jesus to do the impossible? What impact has prayer made in your faith journey?

The disciples headed out to cross the Sea of Galilee and were met by a storm that stopped them in their tracks. They fought to row, but only made it about three miles in the eight or more hours since Jesus had dismissed them. The severe storm hit the boat, tossing the vessel to and fro in the waves. The Greek word *basanizo* used in Matthew 14:24 describes a storm that tortures or causes the boat great distress. Many believe this was more than just a storm, it was an act of God.

2. Read **Matthew 14:25–27**. How did the disciples respond to seeing Jesus? What did the disciples' response reveal about their ability to recognize Jesus in the midst of the storm?

The disciples cried out in fear. They thought they saw a ghost!

3. How did Jesus respond to the disciples? What did Jesus' response reveal about His love for them?

Jesus walking on water is reminiscent of Old Testament descriptions of God walking on water in Job 9:8 and Psalm 77:19. This miraculous act is another instance of Jesus identifying Himself as God.

4. Read **Matthew 14:28, 29**. How did Peter respond to seeing Jesus? What do you think motivated Peter to make this unusual request?

5. Read **Matthew 14:30**. What took Peter's eyes off Jesus? In your everyday life, what tends to distract you from keeping your eyes on Him?

Peter's cry to Jesus reminds us of the psalmist's cry to God in Psalm 69. Peter displayed faith in Jesus when he asked to join Him on the water and also when he cried out for Jesus to save him. However, Jesus still chastised Peter's small amount of faith.

6. Read **Matthew 14:31**. What was Jesus' reply to Peter? How do you think Peter felt after this experience?

7. Read **Matthew 14:32, 33**. What was the disciples' reaction to the multiple miracles they'd just seen? What comfort do you find in seeing another example of Jesus meeting His followers in the midst of a storm?

✤ Personal Challenge

Spend some time making a list of all the storms in your life. You may have broken relationships, financial needs, health issues, and more. After you complete the list, ask Jesus into each of these storms with His healing power.

Faith was crucial throughout the lives of the disciples. As long as Peter was willing to keep his eyes on Jesus, he didn't sink. But as soon as he allowed the storms around him to distract his faith in Jesus, he sank. While Peter failed this test of faith, Jesus still chose to use him. Later, Peter was selected as the one on whom Jesus would build the church.

8. In what areas of your life do you sense Jesus calling you to step out of the boat? What is preventing you from making that courageous step?

Sometimes the storms in life give us the opportunity to grow in our faith. Even when things don't turn out like we expect, if we call out to Jesus in those moments, He reaches out and catches us with His healing hands.

Digging Deeper

Read **Psalm 69**. How would you describe the storm this psalmist faced? What was the central cry of the psalmist's heart? What parallels do you find between the psalmist's cry in Psalm 69 and Peter's cry in Matthew 14:22–33? What do you find helpful from this psalm in keeping your eyes on God in the midst of the storm?

> We have a God who delights in impossibilities.

Andrew Murray,
Christian preacher and author

When You're Desperate

A Woman's Reach

Imagine being a parent whose child is dying. What emotions would you feel?

Jairus, a synagogue leader in Jesus' day, probably feels all of these and more as his only daughter, a small girl of about twelve years old, lies dying. Desperate, Jairus throws himself on the ground at Jesus' feet, begging the miraculous Healer to help his beloved daughter (see Luke 8).

To Jairus's elation, Jesus agrees.

The two begin making their way to Jairus's house, but are held up by a large crowd trying to get to Jesus. Anxious, Jairus pushes and prods the swarms of bodies blocking the route to his daughter.

Blending in with the crowd, one unsuspecting woman weaves her way toward her last hope. She watches the back of Jesus' head like a target as she works her way forward. Finally within arm's length, she stretches out and barely brushes the edge of His cloak.

Power floods out of Jesus and He halts.

Over the hustle and bustle of the crowd, He asks, "Who touched Me?" (v. 45).

His disciple, Peter, snarkily reminds Jesus that He is in the middle of a thick crowd. People are pressing Him on every side. For Him to identify one person's touch is silly.

The woman who brushed the edge of Jesus' cloak knows He is referring to her touch. Overcome with emotion, she once again makes her way toward Jesus and falls at His feet in reverence.

She has spent twelve years suffering from constant bleeding. No amount of doctors, priests, or money has been able to heal her. But by simply touching Jesus' cloak, she has been immediately healed. She can finally return to her family and community without being looked down upon as unclean.

"Do not be afraid; only believe" (Luke 8:50).

After hearing her story, Jesus speaks gentle words she has been waiting to hear for twelve long years: "Daughter, be of good cheer; your faith has made you well. Go in peace" (v. 48).

Before Jesus finishes speaking, a messenger from Jairus's house arrives with horrible news: Jairus's beloved daughter is dead. He tells Jairus to leave Jesus alone; it's too late. Nothing can be done.

But Jesus lends Jairus different advice: "Do not be afraid; only believe" (v. 50).

When they arrive at Jairus's home, Jesus, a few disciples, and Jairus and his wife enter the young girl's room.

Jesus holds her hand and commands her to get up.

The young girl's chest fills with life.

Jairus and his wife cannot believe their eyes. What once was lost is now found. Their beloved daughter is in their arms again.

Anxious to draw Jesus to his daughter's side, Jairus had paused to witness one of Jesus' most amazing miracles—the healing of the woman who suffered from chronic bleeding. With just a touch of Jesus' cloak, her ailment, lasting more than a decade, faded into memory.

As Jairus watched this woman's life be transformed in front of him, he was probably filled with hope and faith that soon Jesus would heal his beloved daughter too. Jesus went above and beyond Jairus's expectations by bringing his daughter back to life.

In the same way, we often have opportunities to watch Jesus meet others in their broken places. When He brings healing and peace to those around us, we can be filled with faith that Jesus will come and enter into our times of brokenness, offering us His healing hands.

Not long after Jesus calmed the storm on the Sea of Galilee, He demonstrated again the importance of faith. Through two miracles—the healing of the hemorrhaging woman and of Jairus's daughter—we find people with great faith who placed their trust in Jesus as Healer. Miracles abounded and lives were changed.

1. Read **Luke 8:40–42**. Many people were crowded around Jesus that day. What made Jairus stand out from the crowd?

Jairus believed that just a touch from Jesus would heal his daughter. As Jesus followed Jairus to his house, He was surrounded by crowds of people. One woman in particular also had the firm belief that a touch from Jesus would heal her of her illness.

2. Read **Luke 8:43–46**. Why do you think Jesus insisted on knowing who touched Him (v. 45)?

While walking through the crowds, Jesus was probably wearing a prayer shawl with blue cords attached to each of the corners, which functioned as a reminder to obey God's commands as laid out in Numbers 15:38, 39. When the woman touched one of the cords from His garment, she was healed in an instant.

3. Read **Mark 5:26**. What detail does the Gospel of Mark add about this woman that isn't included in the Gospel of Luke? Why is this detail significant?

Jewish purity laws rejected women with discharges, like the hemorrhaging woman. She probably spent years as a social outcast and was in desperate need of healing.

4. Read **Luke 8:47, 48**. How did the woman approach Jesus? What did the woman's actions reveal about her faith?

In Luke 8:48, Jesus referred to the woman with a hemorrhage as "Daughter." She was the only woman in Scripture Jesus addressed in this way.

5. Read **Luke 8:49–56**. How were the healings of Jairus's daughter and the hemorrhaging woman similar? How were they different?

Jairus learned that his beloved daughter died. Instead of listening to the bearer of bad news, Jairus turned his eyes and ears to Jesus. Jesus assured Jairus He would heal her.

6. How do you think watching the hemorrhaging woman be healed impacted Jairus's faith for his daughter's healing?

Isaiah 41:10 says, "Fear not, for I am with you; be not dismayed, for I am your God. I will strengthen you, yes, I will help you, I will uphold you with My righteous right hand."

7. Throughout His ministry Jesus met different people in crises. How do difficult times create opportunities for ministry? When in the last year have you been able to encourage someone else because of a similar trial or personal challenge you faced?

✦ Personal Challenge

Spend some time making a list of amazing things you've seen God do in other people's lives. Then, add to the list the amazing things that God has done in your own life. Thank God for each one and allow the stories to strengthen your faith journey. Just as God has provided, strengthened, and protected others, He can do the same for you.

8. Whom do you know in the middle of a crisis right now? How can you pray for him or her and show Jesus' love in a tangible way?

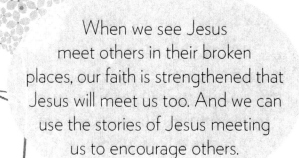

When we see Jesus meet others in their broken places, our faith is strengthened that Jesus will meet us too. And we can use the stories of Jesus meeting us to encourage others.

Digging Deeper

Read **Romans 10:11–13**. How is this passage demonstrated in the story of Jairus and the woman with the issue of blood? How have you experienced this passage to be true in your life? What hope do you find in knowing that those who believe in Christ will not be put to shame?

> Expect great things from God; attempt great things for God.

William Carey,
Father of modern missions

When Everyone Tells You to Be Silent

Bartimaeus

Not too long before entering Jerusalem on Palm Sunday, Jesus and the disciples approach the city of Jericho. Luke 18 paints the picture of a blind man begging along the side of the road. The Gospel of Mark gives the name of this man, Bartimaeus.

Bartimaeus hears the clapping sound of many sandaled feet coming near. He calls out to a passerby in hopes someone will explain why so many people are walking past. A voice from the crowd tells Bartimaeus that Jesus is in their midst. This is the healer that people keep talking about—the man who makes the Jewish authorities so upset because He claims to come in God's name.

Bartimaeus begins to yell. He cries out Jesus' name, screaming for mercy.

Those in the crowd are annoyed by Bartimaeus' shouting and persistence. They try to hush the blind man's pleas, but he only grows louder and louder. Jesus hears Bartimaeus and asks that the blind man be led to Him.

Instead of hobbling to his feet, Bartimaeus leaps up. He doesn't fold up his cloak, but tosses it aside and makes a beeline for Jesus.

As Bartimaeus draws closer, Jesus asks what he wants. Without hesitation, the blind man asks for sight.

With great tenderness, Jesus answers Bartimaeus: "Receive your sight; your faith has made you well" (Luke 18:42).

Immediately, Bartimaeus's eyes are opened. Light pours in and a face sharpens into focus. Not only can he see but he's looking into the face of his healer, Jesus.

"Do not be afraid; only believe" (Luke 8:50).

Bartimaeus's cries for mercy melt into cries of joy and exultation as he praises God. He joins the crowd and begins to follow Jesus. Those who witness the miracle sing praises to God.

Imagine if Bartimaeus would have listened to those trying to hush and silence him. He might never have experienced the miracle and life change Jesus offered him.

When we are in the midst of our broken places, others may try to hush our pursuit of God. Bartimaeus's story reminds us that being bold in our pursuit of Jesus is something to be admired! Even in the midst of our broken places, we can still call out to and pursue Christ—for He longs to offer healing and peace to our lives.

The Gospel of Luke is written as a sort of travelogue, recording the journey of Jesus during His ministry. Luke 18:35 mentions that Jesus was on His way through Jericho, the last leg of His journey into Jerusalem, the city in which He would be crucified. As He reached Jericho, He came across a begging blind man.

1. Read **Luke 18:35–39**. What parallels do you see between the blind man's cry to Jesus and the tax collector's cry in Luke 18:13, 14? What do these passages suggest about our attitude in approaching God?

The blind man heard Jesus was passing by and called Him "Son of David," a first for the Gospel of Luke. This name echoed the Old Testament promise that the Messiah would come through the lineage of King David. The blind man was identifying Jesus as the Messiah and Lord in this passage.

Earlier in the Gospels, the disciples were rebuked by Jesus for dismissing children from Jesus' presence. Similarly, the crowd ignored and hushed the blind man's requests. This trend of silencing the lame, weak, and marginalized was common in Jesus' day. The crowd didn't understand that Jesus didn't hold this same prejudice.

2. What did the blind man's refusal to listen to the rebukes of the crowd reveal about his desire for healing and restoration?

3. In your life, do you tend to approach God out of desperation or out of duty? Explain.

The blind man ignored the crowd's rebukes and continued to call out to Jesus. While he may have been physically blind, he was not blind to the true identity of Jesus—the Messiah. The typical Jewish understanding of the Messiah was a strong and mighty king who would come to sit on the throne. Jesus, however, took time to heal someone considered unworthy. Jesus shattered the mindsets of those around Him by being the Messiah while reaching out to the poor and oppressed.

4. Read **Luke 18:40–43**. Why do you think Jesus asked the blind man what he wanted? (Luke 18:41)

The Gospel of Mark describes the story of Bartimaeus a little differently. In Mark 10:46–52, Bartimaeus threw off his cloak and sprinted to Jesus' side. Nothing was going to stop Bartimaeus from approaching Jesus.

5. How was the blind man's faith displayed throughout this story?

Without touching him, Jesus healed the blind man with words. Jesus' action was reminiscent of His first teaching in Nazareth in Luke 4:18 where He promised the "recovery of sight to the blind." Without even being asked, the once blind man began to follow Jesus. His faith that saved him compelled him to follow the Messiah. Those in the crowd followed suit and began praising God for the miracle.

6. When have you experienced a similar excitement about what God has done in your life?

7. When have you been discouraged by others from pursuing God?

✣ Personal Challenge

Create a prayer bracelet. Gather together your favorite color of ribbon or string and add buttons, washers, or beads. As you create the bracelet, say a specific prayer as you string on each bead or charm. For example, the red bead can be a prayer of thanksgiving for God and His beautiful creation. The pink bead can represent your best friend. Then, each time you wear your new piece of jewelry, be intentional about calling out to Jesus on behalf of yourself and others.

8. What are some ways you can be an encouragement to others who are crying out to God?

Though
others may hush
or discourage us from boldly
seeking God in the midst of our
brokenness, we can still choose to cry
out and pursue Him. Sometimes our
courage will be an inspiration
to others.

Digging Deeper

Read **Matthew 15:25**, **Matthew 17:15**, and **Matthew 20:30**. Compare and contrast the different ways these people cried out to Jesus. What prevents you from crying out to Jesus in freedom? Spend some time prayerfully reflecting on how you can be more open and honest about your need for God in every area of your life.

Wherever redemption is, the light of
revelation abounds.

Patsy Clairmont,
Christian author and speaker

When the Invitation Is Extended

The Final Moment on the Cross

The Gospels of Matthew, Mark, Luke, and John describe the life
and miracles of Jesus. Each perspective uniquely illustrates stories of
Jesus reaching out into the lives of broken people in broken situations
and performing miracles. While these stories of Jesus healing the
broken may vary between gospels, there is one story that is central
in all four gospels: the story of Jesus' death and resurrection.

Throughout His life, Jesus has said many things that allude
to the fact that His end is near. While the disciples still struggle
to grasp what His allusions could mean, Jesus, their Rabbi, is
suddenly arrested during Passover—betrayed by one of their own.

The end Jesus predicted has become reality.

Jesus stands before Pilate, the Roman ruler of the time, on
trial for claiming to be the king of the Jews—essentially claiming

to be God. This supposedly blasphemous claim outrages the Jewish authorities, and they begin planting seeds of hate in the ears of other Jews.

Pilate, not seeing anything illegal according to Roman law, turns Jesus over to the crowd. He asks the crowd what should be done with the man called Jesus. Instead of rescuing their great teacher, the crowd shouts out: Crucify Him!

Jesus is sentenced to death by crucifixion—an excruciating execution involving being nailed to a cross and left to suffocate.

Rather than focusing on the past, Jesus offers hope and new life.

Jesus is whipped and flogged. Onlookers make fun of Him and spit on Him. The guards place robes over His bleeding body and a crown on His head to mock Him. A Roman guard hammers nails through Jesus' wrists and ankles and hoists Him up on the hill.

But Jesus still cries out to God: "Father, forgive them, for they do not know what they do" (v. 34).

Two criminals undergo the same fate as Jesus—left to die on the cross. All three are likely beaten and unrecognizable. From a distance, nothing separates two common criminals from the Savior of the world except the signs describing their crimes hung above them. Jesus' reads, "THIS IS THE KING OF THE JEWS" (v. 38).

Pilate could have had it written that Jesus claimed to be the King of the Jews, but instead he states the claim as truth.

One criminal calls out to Jesus, mocking Him like the others. Before Jesus has the chance to respond, the second criminal comes to His defense.

The second criminal pleads with Jesus and, between heavy breaths, asks Him to remember him. The invitation to know Christ is accepted. The criminal repents and asks for forgiveness. This criminal has nothing to gain by defending Jesus because they are all headed to a predictable end. Yet he has everything to gain through Jesus, the King of the Jews.

Jesus cries out, "Today you will be with Me in Paradise" (v. 43).

Jesus meets the criminal in the midst of his brokenness and welcomes him into His kingdom. Jesus shares in the darkest day of the man sentenced to death next to Him. Rather than focusing on the past, Jesus offers hope and new life. Jesus forgives him and welcomes him into His kingdom—a place of new life and hope.

Jesus extends the same invitation to all of us no matter what we've been through or what we've done. Nothing is beyond God's redemption, restoration, or healing. Even when all hope seems lost, God opens His arms wide and extends an invitation into His kingdom by believing in Him.

After spending time hanging out with His disciples, Jesus was confronted on the Mount of Olives and betrayed. One of Jesus' own disciples, Judas Iscariot, handed his teacher over to the Jewish authorities for a bag of silver. Jesus was arrested and sent to the Roman ruler, Pilate, who debated whether or not to punish Jesus. Three times he asked the crowd what should be done with Jesus. Each time the crowd called for Jesus' crucifixion. Pilate released a convicted murderer and sent a sinless Jesus to His death.

1. Read **Luke 23:1–25**. Why do you think Pilate finally handed Jesus over to be crucified?

Jesus died as a sacrifice for our sins. During His hours on the cross, He bore the sins of the world on His shoulders so that we are able to have an active relationship with God. Talk about bringing healing through broken places!

2. Many traditions recognize the seven last sayings of Jesus throughout the Gospels. In the chart below, record each of Jesus' last sayings. Place a star next to the verse that encourages you most.

Verse	Jesus' Saying
Luke 23:34	
Luke 23:43	
John 19:26	
Matthew 27:46; Mark 15:34	
John 19:28	
John 19:30	
Luke 23:46	

The theme of forgiveness weaves throughout Luke's gospel. During Jesus' death, He went as far to forgive those who were putting Him through such pain and agony.

3. Read **Luke 23:26–34**. How did Jesus respond to those who were mocking and abusing Him? When have you found yourself in a situation where you were mocked or belittled? How did you respond to the situation?

4. What conditions did Jesus place on His forgiveness of others in Luke 23:34? How would your relationships with others be different if you practiced this kind of outrageous forgiveness?

In Matthew 5:44, Jesus challenged us, "Love your enemies . . . and pray for those who spitefully use you and persecute you." When we forgive those who have wronged us, we offer healing to lives and relationships. Just as we need healing in our own lives, we need to offer healing in the lives of those around us.

5. In the space below, write down the name of someone who needs forgiveness or relationships that need healing. Over the next week, prayerfully consider how you can work toward bringing healing in their lives.

Jesus offered another example of forgiveness toward someone who seemed unworthy. Luke 23:43 is often remembered as Jesus' saying of salvation. A criminal that was sentenced to death cried out to Jesus in his darkest moment. In turn, Jesus reached out to the criminal and offered hope and healing.

6. The two criminals in Luke 23:39–43 confronted Jesus differently. How did each one approach Jesus? How do you identify with each of these criminals?

7. What does Jesus' response to the crucified criminal teach us about salvation?

✤ Personal Challenge

Pull out the prayer journal you began during chapter one. Read through and pray over the various prayers that are left unanswered. Praise God for the prayers that have been answered. Celebrate the fact that when you call out to God in broken places, He will meet you and offer His healing hands.

Jesus' life didn't end on the cross. Three days later, Jesus rose from the grave, giving hope and life to all who believe—even those who seem unworthy, like the criminal on the cross.

8. What areas of your life are currently in need of Jesus' healing power? Spend time lifting up those situations, relationships, and hardships in prayer with joyful expectation for God to answer.

The invitation to believe in Jesus Christ as the Savior of the world extends to everyone. No matter what you've been through or experienced, Jesus waits— arms wide open—for you to believe in Him and experience the fullness of healing and restoration in your life.

Digging Deeper

Jesus' death is not the end of the story! Read **Luke 24**, which describes what happened after Jesus died on the cross. If Jesus could overcome death on a cross, how much more willing are you to trust Him during your broken moments? How are you comforted by the hope in Christ from Luke 24?

Leader's Guide

Chapter 1: When the Storms of Life Roll In

Calming the Storm

Focus: No matter what stormy situation you're facing, you can be encouraged that no difficulty is more powerful than God.

1. Whether due to the loss of a job, a financial hardship, or crumbling relationship, the storms of life can cause a plethora of emotions like anger, confusion, or grief.

2. As a leader, consider setting the tone and level of intimacy by offering your response first. Be gentle in requesting others to respond as wounds from these events may still be raw, and memories, painful. Be sure to limit answers to one sentence or phrase. For some not to have noticed Christ's role during this period is not unusual. Some participants may have incredible stories of redemption and healing, while others may not. Church, friends, family, reading Scripture, or even smaller things such as the comfort of a pet may have made a difference through those difficult times.

3. Scripture says she got up and began to wait on Jesus. In response to Jesus' healing, Peter's mother-in-law began serving Him. Many will respond with praise, thanksgiving, or service just like Peter's mother-in-law. Sometimes we can become caught up in the calmed storms and forget to show any gratitude at all. Encourage the participants to be proactive in thanking the Lord for the calmed storms (past and present) in their lives.

4. Verse 16 says the spirits were driven out with a word. Jesus clearly has complete power over evil.

5. The disciples were so scared of the storm they thought they were going to die, while Jesus slept right through. Jesus rebuked the wind and the waves, showing His power over the storm. Both the disciples and Jesus knew He had the ability to stop the tempest.

6. Answers will vary as participants reconcile which category their issues fall into. Some may struggle with disease and illness in themselves or a loved one. Others may be dealing with the effects of a tornado or hurricane. Understand that no matter what category an issue falls under or even if it doesn't fit into a category, God has power over everything.

7. Jonah 1:5 says the sailors were afraid as they cried out to their own gods. This is similar to Matthew 8:25 where the disciples showed fear and cried out to Jesus. After the storms were calmed in both stories, both the sailors and the disciples began to understand who controls nature (Jonah 1:16 and Matthew 8:27).

8. Not everyone will remember a story when his or her storms were calmed in an instant. Examples include times when financial burdens were alleviated, homes were sold, healing abounded, and relationships were mended. Encourage participants to look for moments where God calmed a storm quickly—offering hope and strengthening faith.

Digging Deeper

The Mark account says where Jesus slept on the boat. The Mark account also records different words of the disciples when they woke Jesus and what Jesus said to rebuke the storm. The Luke account adds some setting to the event and also records the danger they were facing. The disciples sounded angry toward Jesus in the Mark account. This may be comforting to some participants. We gain new insight into the story with three different perspectives of the same event.

Chapter 2: When You're Between a Rock and a Hard Place

Tax Time

Focus: God is not only with you but goes before you in whatever situation you're facing. You can trust Jesus with your needs and know He hears you.

1. Our faith is constantly changing—growing and stretching as we continue to get to know God. There are so many facets of His character that are being discovered daily. As we continue on the road to knowing Jesus, we may find our faith growing without our even realizing it.

2. As the disciples witnessed Jesus' transfiguration and His miracles, their faith was likely strengthened. They began to see His identity revealed through these various experiences in Matthew 17. Through these miracles, they saw that Jesus was the Messiah—the Savior and King sent by God— who was coming to save His people.

3. Sometimes answers to our problems or issues present themselves before we even go to God in prayer.

4. Jesus asked Peter: "What do you think, Simon?" and "From whom do the kings of the earth take customs or taxes, from their sons or from strangers?" Jesus may have been asking Peter's opinion to bring him in on the conversation or to solidify what Jesus was about to do. Peter's answer was an interesting revelation of who Jesus was. Because Jesus was the Son of God, His Father was God—the one in charge of the temple. Therefore, Jesus (by relation) and His followers (part of Jesus' family) were actually exempt from the temple tax.

Passage	Who God Asked	What God Asked
Genesis 3:1–10	Adam (the man)	Where are you?
Genesis 4:1–8	Cain	Why are you angry? And why has your countenance fallen?
Genesis 18:1–15	Abraham	Why did Sarah laugh, saying, "Shall I surely bear a child, since I am old?"
Exodus 4:1–5	Moses	What is that in your hand?

5. Adam had to admit his error and reveal himself to the Lord. Cain had to admit that his offering wasn't as pleasing as his brother's. Abraham had to answer to his wife's lack of faith in the situation. Moses had to trust that God would reveal Himself to Pharaoh, the Egyptian king.

6. Spend time sharing stories of God's miraculous provision in the lives of your participants. God often requires work from us to accomplish His miracles.

7. Answers will vary.

8. Spend time in prayer asking God in what areas of life He is calling you to action. The response may be as simple as befriending a neighbor or financially supporting a child across the world. Ask God to put situations in your path that allow you to participate in God's plan for the world around you.

Digging Deeper

Humility is an act of obedience to the Lord. Psalm 31 says that those who are faithful, the humble, are preserved, but those who are proud are paid back in full for their pride. Often we can allow our pride to get in the way of how God works in our lives. We desire the credit, instead of handing it over to God.

Chapter 3: When You're Physically and Spiritually Hungry
More Than Enough

Focus: Sometimes when we find ourselves in the middle of a great need, we can become so focused on what we need, we miss the fact that God wants to give us the greatest gift of all—Himself! Whatever brokenness you're experiencing, rest assured God wants to give you an abundance of His presence.

1. Often, since we easily see how we are getting along physically, we forget about our spiritual hunger. We may find ourselves spiritually sustained as we dive into God's Word daily, spend time with those who encourage us in faith, or remain in constant communication with Jesus through prayer. When we forget to do these things, we may find our spiritual gauges on empty.

2. As your group shares its fulfilling spiritual disciplines, consider asking the participants to practice one of them as a group during a set amount of time. Encourage one another to journal during the journey and gauge your spiritual tanks throughout. A great book to read on this subject is *Celebration of Discipline* by Richard Foster.

3. We live in an age of busyness. As we pack our schedules full of church activities, exercise, carpooling, working, and spending time with our family, spiritual practices tend to fall by the wayside. Encourage your participants to set aside ten minutes each morning or evening to spend practicing a spiritual discipline. This will look different for each participant since schedules and alertness vary throughout the day, but love, grace, and patience increase when we make time to nourish our relationship with God each day.

4. Philip saw the impossibility of the situation at hand—feeding that large of a crowd would have been impossible without it costing a fortune. Andrew offered the lunch of a boy, five loaves and two fish.

5. The disciples had no idea what was going to happen. They saw the large crowd and the small portions of fish and bread and couldn't wrap their minds around how Jesus expected them to feed the crowd. In the same way, God may be asking us to do big things that seem impossible or improbable. Remember that God wants to use us as an instrument to care and provide for others. He will find a way. We need only to be obedient and willing.

6. Encourage participants to recall a time when God provided above and beyond their greatest imaginations. This could be through finances or abundant friendships. When we see the areas where God provides for us lavishly, our faith tends to increase as we place our trust in God who provides abundantly.

7. The Jews recognized that Jesus gave them a meal, but didn't understand Jesus was offering them more than just physical bread. Many believed Jesus to be another prophet, like Elijah, not the actual Messiah. The Jews only saw the bread, not the Sustainer and Messiah who gave them the bread. Often, it may be easy for us to feel the same way as the Jews— only seeing the blessings and never recognizing the Blesser. Jesus not only wants to fulfill our physical needs, but our spiritual needs. His desire is to fill us so we will never hunger or thirst again.

8. We may often disqualify ourselves from getting involved where God wants to use us. We might feel reluctant to be obedient to His plan for us because we don't have the best to offer. We may be too busy, not gifted in an area, or not ready to take that leap. God wants to use us as His instrument no matter our abilities, gifts, or talents. When we are obedient to Him, we'll be surprised at the amazing ways God uses us. We may find ourselves reluctant or hesitant to offer our time, treasures, or talents to

be used by God because they don't seem to be good enough. This week, spend time praying for God to open your eyes and heart to ways He can use you despite inadequacies.

Digging Deeper

God told Moses that He would rain down bread on the people in the mornings and provide meat in the evening. The people gathered just the right amount to satisfy themselves. This was the same as the bread and meat provided to the multitude. Reflect on the ways Jesus has shown Himself to provide both physically and spiritually in your own life.

Chapter 4: When You've Lost Your Most Precious
A Widow's Son

Focus: As Jesus walked into the widow's moment of great pain and loss, He also wants to walk into our moments of pain and loss with the intention of offering hope and life.

1. Jesus was filled with compassion toward the woman. Not only did He tell her not to cry, He gave her a reason to stop—by raising her son to life. Jesus doesn't offer empty promises or words to us during our times of need. Instead, His words are filled with love, grace, and compassion.

2. When we cultivate compassion, we find that prayer for others flows naturally. We feel their pain and hardships and speak to the Lord on their behalf. Romans 8:26, 27 assures us that even when we don't know what to pray for, the Spirit intercedes on our behalf. When we cultivate compassion, our friendships and relationships with others strengthen greatly. We are more willing to offer a helping hand and show grace and love to those who are in need. As we feel others' pain and areas of needs through compassion, we become willing to do whatever it takes to show them love. Usually, this love is expressed through serving. By making

dinner for a busy mom, cleaning a widow's home, or offering to volunteer for a local community service project, you are putting your compassion into action.

3. This can be as simple as offering free-of-charge babysitting to a single mom or stopping to give a meal certificate to a homeless person. Examples could include any time our time, money, or energy is given to help someone else. When we take risks to help someone in need, we are putting him or her above ourselves.

4. The witnesses were filled with awe and praised God. They spread the news about Jesus all over the countryside.

5. Spend time sharing your favorite verses as a group—whichever scriptures have encouraged or restored you over the last month. Some favorites may include Psalm 139, John 14:6, Jeremiah 29:11, or Zephaniah 3:17.

6. Answers

Scripture	Power of Hope
1 John 3:3	It purifies us, just as He is pure.
Psalm 31:24	Be of good courage.
Psalm 42:11	Instead of being cast down and disquieted, put your hope in God.
Psalm 71:5	The Lord is our trust.

7. Answers will vary. Encourage participants to share other passages they may love that express the power of hope.

8. God desires to bring us new life. Spend time in prayer asking God to reveal areas in your life that need restoration and healing. Pray for the courage to give those areas to God.

Digging Deeper

In both cases, the widow's son died. Both Jesus and Elijah touched the dead bodies and gave the living sons back to their mothers. Both stories resulted in people believing. In 1 Kings, the widow actually blamed Elijah for her son's death. Elijah spoke more than just a sentence to resurrect the son. Jesus didn't call out to God to resurrect the body, but instead spoke directly to the body—this demonstrates that He was more than a prophet but the Son of God. Jesus has authority over everything—including death.

Chapter 5: When All Hope Is Lost

Lazarus

Focus: When we experience betrayal, loss, and death, Jesus mourns with us. We need not fear death because Jesus is the resurrection and the life.

1. Scripture says Jesus loved Martha, Mary, and Lazarus. The relationship was probably a deep and loving friendship.

2. Jesus said that what happened to Lazarus would glorify God. Jesus didn't rush to dying Lazarus's side because He knew he would be resurrected to give God glory.

3. Jesus told Martha that Lazarus would rise again, but Martha didn't understand. She believed Jesus was the Son of God, but didn't know how Jesus would fix the situation at hand.

4. Jesus doesn't only claim to be able to create new life by resurrecting the dead, but He is also offering new eternal life to those who believe in Him. They who trust will have life spiritually, even though they may die physically.

5. Jesus did not grieve over Lazarus's death because He lost a friend. Instead, He grieved over the effect of sin and death on the whole world. He also noticed the pain and grief on the faces of Mary and Martha and expressed His love for them through tears.

6. Raising Lazarus from the dead was seemingly impossible to the onlookers and Martha. Their concerns and protests were valid in their circumstance. We forget Jesus can do anything and has control over every area of life. We may also view impossible situations as hopeless, like the onlookers and Martha did.

7. Answers

Psalm 49:15: "But God will redeem my soul from the power of the grave, for He shall receive me."

John 5:21: "For as the Father raises the dead and gives life to them, even so the Son gives life to whom He will."

John 5:25: "Most assuredly, I say to you, the hour is coming, and now is, when the dead will hear the voice of the Son of God; and those who hear will live."

John 6:40: "And this is the will of Him who sent Me, that everyone who sees the Son and believes in Him may have everlasting life; and I will raise him up at the last day."

John 11:25: "Jesus said to her, 'I am the resurrection and the life. He who believes in Me, though he may die, he shall live.'"

Acts 26:8: "Why should it be thought incredible by you that God raises the dead?"

2 Corinthians 1:9: "Yes, we had the sentence of death in ourselves, that we should not trust in ourselves but in God who raises the dead."

2 Corinthians 4:14: "Knowing that He who raised up the Lord Jesus will also raise us up with Jesus, and will present us with you."

8. Spend time asking God to reveal names and faces of those in your life who need a friend in their time of pain or loss. Consider all the ways you can show compassion and love to those people. This week, find one way to show compassion to one of these people. Cook her a meal, take her to coffee, clean her house, or offer a free night of babysitting. Sometimes even a little gesture of compassion can mean a lot.

Digging Deeper

Jesus isn't just able to empathize with us in weaknesses, but has actually experienced every temptation and overcome each one. Often when we lose a loved one or go through a time of grief we are more understanding of others who experience similar pain.

Chapter 6: When Everyone Turns Their Back on You
The Man-Born-Blind

Focus: Jesus longs to bring more than physical healing to our lives; He wants to bring healing to every aspect of our lives, no matter what challenges we're facing.

1. Often, we can get so caught up in the theological correctness of Scripture we miss out on the bigger picture.

2. An initial reading of Jesus' response may strike many as cruel or thoughtless. Jesus said the man was born in suffering in order to glorify God in his healing.

3. Jesus asked the blind man to wash in the Pool of Siloam. The blind man agreed and did as he was told. His obedience led to his healing. The man-born-blind demonstrated faith in Jesus in his willingness to obey.

4. Neighbors and those who knew the blind man didn't recognize him immediately. They couldn't believe the man before them was the same

man. Some of his friends and neighbors probably couldn't fathom such a miracle in their heads, and therefore denied the wonder completely. Others could accept a miracle took place and believed the man was who he said he was.

5. The Pharisees questioned the legitimacy of the miracle and of Jesus. They did not believe the man-born-blind, so they questioned his parents. Allow participants to share controversies they may have experienced in their ministries, small groups, or churches. Approach this question with gentleness, as some wounds may still be new and raw. Answers may include anything from theological disagreements to different interpretations of Scripture.

6. The blind man's parents seemed to avoid the Pharisees' confrontation at all costs. Rather than standing up for their son and rejoicing in the miracle, they feared what the Pharisees would do. This may have been frustrating, disheartening, or understandable to the man-born-blind.

7. Even when we feel rejected, we're still pursued and loved wholeheartedly by Jesus. He desires to pursue us and remove the areas of spiritual blindness in our lives, no matter what others may think of us.

8. Spend time praying for the person in your life who feels isolated and alone. Ask God to give you the discernment and wisdom as to how best to be a source of encouragement and comfort to him or her during the week.

Digging Deeper

In Mark 8:22–26, Mark records the story of Jesus healing a blind man in Bethsaida. Jesus took the man by hand and also spit on the man's eyes. Jesus put His hands over the man's eyes twice and he was healed. In Matthew 9:27–31, Jesus healed two blind men by touching their eyes. Matthew 20:29–34 sounds very similar to the account in Matthew 9, but the two men immediately followed Jesus after they were healed. Luke 4:18

and Isaiah 35:5 point to the Messiah as the person who recovers the sight of the blind. By healing the blind, Jesus revealed that He was the one they had been waiting for.

Chapter 7: When You're at the End of Your Rope
A Huge Catch of Fish

Focus: When you feel like you're at the end of your rope, God will meet you there—sometimes in the most surprising ways. Such moments become opportunities for greater discipleship and obedience, as well as opportunities to impact the lives of others.

1. Everyday situations can make us feel at the end of our rope. We may be caught in financial strains, the unknowns of a mysterious illness, the pains of a broken relationship, loss of patience with coworkers, or discouragement because of the lack of productivity during a day.

2. A skilled fisherman by profession, Simon Peter acknowledged Jesus' authority by calling him "Master" in verse 5. The disciples obeyed Jesus' instructions. While they may still have doubted they would catch anything, they showed trust by letting down the nets one last time.

3. Simon Peter fell to his knees and stated that he was a sinner. All of his companions on the boat were astonished by the miracle. Our reactions may be similar to the disciples'. We may find ourselves humbled and feel undeserving. Others may only feel shocked and astonished by God's powerful presence.

4. Often we can get caught up in the moment, assuming God meeting our needs is the end of the story instead of the beginning of something new He has for us. As demonstrated in the lives of the disciples, God can meet our needs as an invitation to a greater life of obedience—affecting

countless others. God steps into those moments not merely for us but to impact others.

5. The stories are similar in that the disciples spent all night fishing with no results. Jesus was unknown to the disciples in both instances, but they still obeyed. The catch of fish was miraculous in both situations. Some may be surprised that Jesus was unrecognizable to the disciples since they had spent several years following Him around and learning from Him. One might think that they would be able to recognize Him. However, the disciples weren't expecting to see Jesus, as He had already died and been resurrected.

6. Peter denied even knowing Jesus three times, just as Jesus predicted (see John 18:15–27). He may no longer have felt worthy to be considered one of Jesus' disciples. He left his life of discipleship and returned to what he knew best: fishing. Jesus went out of His way to make sure Peter knew His love and the plan Jesus had for him. Jesus loves us in the same pursuing way He loved Peter; He is faithful even when we are faithless.

7. Jesus asked Peter the same question three times. In response to Peter's answer, Jesus said, "Feed My lambs," "Tend My sheep," and "Feed My sheep." These were invitations to shepherd or pastor others. He again told Peter and the other disciples to follow Him—a call for renewed discipleship.

8. There may be several areas in our lives where God is calling us to greater discipleship. Encourage participants to spend time in prayer asking God for discernment in their lives.

Digging Deeper

Isaiah and Simon Peter responded in similar ways. They both felt inadequate to be in the presence of the Lord because they were unclean (or sinners). Often when we look at the pure love God shows us, we become aware of our own inadequacies. Sometimes, we may find ourselves admiring the vastness of the mountains or the beauty of a sunrise and be reminded of the character of God—His power, grace, beauty, and strength. This may evoke humility in our hearts as we understand our deep need for Him as our Savior.

Chapter 8: When You Need Healing

Ten People with Leprosy

Focus: Whenever Jesus meets us in our brokenness, we have the opportunity to express gratitude through thanksgiving and praise.

1. They cried out: "Jesus, Master, have mercy on us!" Whether in times of illness, a struggling relationship, or an overwhelming day, we can all relate to being at the end of our rope and crying out to God for mercy.

2. This person with leprosy recognized that Jesus was the reason for his healing. He came back to Him and began to praise God. He threw himself at Jesus' feet and thanked Him. The man with leprosy probably knew there was nothing he could say or do to show Jesus how grateful he was. He could then return to his family and community.

3. When God answers big prayers in our lives we are often moved to worship Him. Others may see every day as an opportunity to passionately worship God.

4. Jesus asked: "Were there not ten cleansed?" "But where are the nine?" and "Were there not any found who returned to give glory to God except this foreigner?" Jesus expected all ten men to return to thank Him for healing them of leprosy.

5. Often we may feel entitled to or expectant of certain things. This attitude can lead to ingratitude. In seasons of busyness, we may let gratitude slip from our minds.

6. Answers

Scripture	Importance of Gratitude
Psalm 100:1–5	God made us and we are His; therefore; we are to be thankful.
1 Chronicles 16:8–12	God continues to perform miracles and wonders on our behalf; praise Him for it.
Philippians 1:3–7	Praise God for friendships.
1 Corinthians 4:7	Be thankful for who you are and what you are given.
1 Thessalonians 5:18	Gratitude is God's will for us.
Hebrews 13:15	Gratitude is our sacrifice to God.

7. Answers will vary. We can be thankful for Christ's sacrifice, for blessing us, or for providing us with families or a great job.

8. Becoming intentional about thankfulness is a tough task. Think of cues that remind you to thank God for things in your life. For example, every time you drive by a school or school bus, thank God for your family. Every time you hear a dog bark, thank God for His creation. Each time you open your inbox at work, take a minute to thank God for His provision. Small cues can help us develop an attitude of gratitude.

Digging Deeper

Encourage participants to be creative in their writing of Psalm 150. Ask the group what words they can rhyme or what other scriptures they can weave in for an extra challenge.

Chapter 9: When God Asks You to Step Out of the Boat
Walking on Water

Focus: Sometimes the storms in life give us the opportunity to grow in our faith. Even when things don't turn out like we expect, if we call out to Jesus in those moments, He reaches out and catches us with His healing hands.

1. Jesus was a man of prayer. As we saw in chapter three, when He multiplied the meal for the five thousand, He prayed. Prayer is our way to communicate with God. If we don't communicate with our closest friends, we probably don't have a very intimate relationship. In the same way, if we are in prayer often, we are able to have a closer, more intimate relationship with God.

2. The disciples responded like many normal people would: they were terrified. They assumed the figure walking toward them was a ghost. In the midst of the storm, all the disciples focused on was their fear. They didn't even notice their loving teacher walking out to them.

3. Jesus gently assured and calmed their fear by revealing His identity to them.

4. Peter responded by asking Jesus to order him to walk on the water also. Peter had full faith that Jesus was able to not only walk on water Himself but to enable Peter to do the same.

5. Peter became distracted by the storm raging around him. Often the storms in our lives cause us to take our focus off of Jesus.

6. Jesus immediately reached out and caught Peter. He asked him why he doubted. Peter probably was reassured in that moment that the figure was in fact Jesus, but also discouraged that he lacked faith.

7. The disciples worshiped Jesus and knew that He was the Son of God. Jesus has full control over storms in the world—physical, spiritual, and emotional. He chose to go out and meet His disciples in the midst of these.

8. Encourage participants to listen for those areas in which Jesus is calling them out of the boat. Encourage them to step out and follow His calling in faith.

Digging Deeper

The psalmist describes a terrifying storm that threatened his life. The cry central to the psalmist's heart is God—he seeks that God will save him.

Chapter 10: When You're Desperate

A Woman's Reach

Focus: When we see Jesus meet someone in his or her broken places, our faith is strengthened that Jesus will meet us too. And we can use the stories of Jesus meeting us to encourage others.

1. Jairus was probably a well-known leader in the community. He came and fell at Jesus' feet, begging for help.

2. Jesus felt the power go out from Him. He wanted to know if this woman had the faith to admit she touched Him and proclaim her healing.

3. Mark adds that the woman spent all she had on doctors to try to get better, but her efforts only made the problem worse. This proves that her illness was an incurable disease. While countless doctors couldn't heal her, one touch from Jesus stopped her bleeding.

4. The woman fell at Jesus' feet. She displayed her great faith by proclaiming what Jesus had done for her.

5. Jesus brought His healing touch to two seemingly impossible situations: a woman who had an incurable illness and a daughter who had died. In both situations, Jesus healed. An entire crowd saw the hemorrhaging woman healed, whereas Jesus was exclusive in who could see Jairus's daughter being healed. The woman had suffered with the illness for twelve years—the age of Jairus's daughter. They were at different ends of the socioeconomic spectrum. Jairus and his family were well-known

in society, but the woman had been an outcast from the temple since the start of her illness.

6. Jairus probably watched in awe as the woman was healed—ecstatic that this man could also heal his beloved daughter.

7. Jairus and the hemorrhaging woman were desperate. Jesus was their only hope. As they placed their trust in Him, He was faithful to meet them in their brokenness and healed their situations. Encourage participants to share a specific example of using their own places of loss and difficulty that God has brought them through to reach others.

8. Encourage participants to extend love and meet the physical needs of those who are desperate. Consider making them a meal or taking them out to coffee. As we become the hands and feet of Jesus, we are able to show His love to those in need.

Digging Deeper

Jairus was a man of high stature in the community. He approached Jesus in humility but with no shame. The woman, on the other hand, was an outcast in society and snuck up to Jesus to receive healing. However, Jesus extended healing to both people because of their faith.

Chapter 11: When Everyone Tells You to Be Silent
Bartimaeus

Focus: Though others may hush or discourage us from boldly seeking God in the midst of our brokenness, we can still choose to cry out and pursue Him. Sometimes our courage will be an inspiration to others.

1. Both men cried out to Jesus for mercy. These passages describe a humble approach to God; we are sinners and are in need of mercy.

2. The blind man was adamant about being healed. He disregarded the voices of those around him and kept shouting toward Jesus.

3. Answers will vary. Depending on the circumstance, we may find ourselves approaching God out of desperation or duty.

4. Rather than healing him immediately, Jesus probably wanted the crowd to see and be amazed by the man's boldness. The man was brave enough to ask for his sight, and Jesus was powerful enough to give vision to him.

5. The blind man had faith that Jesus would heal him—so he called out to Him in boldness.

6. When we see God work in powerful ways in our lives, many times we also respond with praise. The excitement bubbles over into words of thanksgiving and praise to God.

7. Answers will vary. Approach this question in gentleness, as there may be many who have been hurt by others and are only now beginning to pursue God. Celebrate their active choice to pursue Him.

8. Rather than hush those who are crying out to God, encourage them! Join them in prayer and cry out to God on their behalf.

Digging Deeper

The woman in Matthew 15 knelt before Jesus and said, "Lord, help me!" The man in Matthew 17 called upon the Lord for mercy toward his son. In Matthew 20, two blind men called Jesus the Son of David and cried out for mercy. Answers will vary.

Chapter 12: When the Invitation Is Extended

The Final Moment on the Cross

Focus: The invitation to believe in Jesus Christ as the Savior of the world extends to everyone. No matter what you've been through or experienced, Jesus waits—arms wide open—for you to believe in Him and experience the fullness of healing and restoration in your life.

1. Jesus had to die as an atoning sacrifice for our sins. Pilate debated whether or not to send Him to be crucified, but ultimately gave in to the cries of the crowd. Even through this, Pilate did the will of God.

2. Answers

Verse	Jesus' Saying
Luke 23:34	"Father, forgive them, for they do not know what they do."
Luke 23:43	"Assuredly, I say to you, today you will be with Me in Paradise."
John 19:26	"Woman, behold your son!"
Matthew 27:46; Mark 15:34	"My God, My God, why have You forsaken Me?"
John 19:28	"I thirst!"
John 19:30	"It is finished!"
Luke 23:46	"Father, 'into Your hands I commit My spirit.'"

3. Jesus didn't respond with anger or criticism. Instead Jesus pled with His Father on behalf of those who were against Him—praying for them and forgiving them. Answers will vary.

4. Jesus didn't place any conditions on forgiveness—He extended forgiveness freely. In Luke 23:34 He says, "Father, forgive them, for they do not know what they do." Answers will vary. Often forgiving those who have wronged us can be very difficult. However, if we truly were to practice the forgiveness Jesus offers, we would have a world with much less pain, brokenness, and hurt.

5. Approach this question carefully in group discussion. As all situations are different, there is no sure process when it comes to forgiveness. Remind participants that when we receive the healing power of Jesus, we are able to offer it to others. What a freeing ability!

6. The first criminal mocked Jesus. The second criminal defended Jesus and asked Him to remember him when He entered His kingdom. Often times we may find ourselves like the first criminal—doubting Jesus' power and challenging His authority. We cry out wondering why the God of the universe can't act in ways we decide. Other times we may approach Jesus humbly and cry out to Him in our brokenness like the second criminal.

7. Jesus' response teaches us that no matter where we've been or what we've done, the invitation to believe in Him extends to us. We are never— even at the last moments of our lives—beyond God's saving grace.

8. Spend time as a group praying over these requests. Encourage participants to lift up their requests to the Lord. Even as the group finishes this study, continue to check in on these requests over the next few weeks and the months ahead.

Digging Deeper

Jesus overcame death and rose from the dead. The hope illustrated in Luke 24 embodies the restoration Jesus desires for each of us in our own lives.

About the Author

A popular speaker at churches and leading conferences such as Catalyst and Thrive, Margaret Feinberg was recently named one of the 30 Emerging Voices who will help lead the church in the next decade by *Charisma* magazine. She has written more than two dozen books and Bible studies, including the critically acclaimed *The Organic God, The Sacred Echo, Scouting the Divine,* and their corresponding DVD Bible studies. She is known for her relational teaching style and inviting people to discover the relevance of God and His Word in a modern world.

Margaret and her books have been covered by national media, including CNN, the Associated Press, *Los Angeles Times,* Dallas Morning News, *Washington Post, Chicago Tribune,* and many others. She currently lives in Colorado with her 6'8" husband, Leif, and superpup, Hershey. Go ahead, become her friend on Facebook, follow her on Twitter @mafeinberg, add her on Google+, or check out her website at www.margaretfeinberg.com.

CPSIA information can be obtained at www.ICGtesting.com
Printed in the USA
LVOW12s1737280713

344813LV00009B/51/P